D1368429

Our Animal Neighbors

Books by Alan Devoe

PHUDD HILL

DOWN TO EARTH

SPEAKING OF ANIMALS

LIVES AROUND US

THIS FASCINATING ANIMAL WORLD

OUR ANIMAL NEIGHBORS

Our
Animal Neighbors

by ALAN DEVOE
with MARY BERRY DEVOE
illustrated by Walter Ferguson

NEW YORK   TORONTO   LONDON

McGRAW-HILL BOOK COMPANY, INC.

OUR ANIMAL NEIGHBORS

Library of Congress Catalog Card Number: 53-5185

The author wishes to express thanks to the *American Mercury*, for permission to use in adapted form passages dealing with psychology and animal behavior; to *Audubon Magazine*, for the use of brief excerpts in Chapters 2, 4, and 5; and to the *Catholic World*, for permission to retell in abridgment the anecdote of the fox-game in Chapter 9.

PUBLISHED BY THE MCGRAW-HILL BOOK COMPANY, INC.

PRINTED IN THE UNITED STATES OF AMERICA

Contents

The Neighborhood

Just as these words were begun, Mary ran to our big northeast window—the one that looks directly into the woods, where the old wood road comes winding down—and called that there was a doe just there, looking in upon us, with what looked to be a last May's fawn beside her. We have been staring out, with our noses against the glass, at these two tawny neighbors of ours standing there looking in. They are still there as this writing resumes. I don't know how many scores of deer—or is it hundreds?—Mary and I have known intimately in this neighborhood of ours; but we go on continually with our learning. We have just gone on some more with it now. While we watched the doe, so close outside the window glass that when she raised her head we could see the dark penciling around her eyes and her breath fogging the pane, she pawed something up from the grass and munched it with relish. It was a pocked and time-grayed fragment of suet, long left there for the chickadees. So we know something now about our neighbor, the deer, that isn't the kind of thing you are likely to learn in any way except by the close and continual intercourse of neighborliness. Our vegetarian friend and neighbor Whitetail, when the mood is mysteriously upon her, will eat a bit of meat.

This neighborhood of ours holds about a hundred and twenty-five acres, "be the same more or less," as the deed makers used to be fond of putting it in their by-guess-and-by-God way. Within this area it has something of the diversity of the macrocosm. A part of our neighborhood, the greater part, is wooded hills, long-lying, gently rounded hills, the tipmost top of the highest part being a thousand feet or so above sea level. There is plenty of high acreage of hemlock-dense woodedness to afford good sheltering place for white-tailed deer and good prowling place sometimes for a bobcat neighbor. Then the hills, as they slope downward and southward, change from woodedness to sunny, open uplands and then change again to forty acres or so of bottom-land pasture

The Neighborhood

through which about a half-mile of brook runs crookedly. It was all a farmstead once upon a time, but not in many years; and in any case the most assiduous farming of such a patch of the planet as this could never do much more than level and tame the bottom-land part of the acreage a bit and clear somewhat the steep hillsides. This once farmstead, that has now been our neighborhood for nearly all our lives together, remains in many ways not significantly different from what it was in that far-away long ago when no human feet walked it except, perhaps, an occasional straying brown pair belonging to one of the Wawyochtonock Indians, the "people of the curving channel."

From the time we first saw it, we loved it for its diversity—this uncommon gathering, in one boundaried neighborhood of a hundred and some acres, of evergreen woods and oak woods and a curious deep-wooded glen or ravine, in combination with open lands, meadows, and the long, winding brook for herons, muskrats, and frog-hunting coons. People live where they live for a variety of reasons; but what is loveliest to us is the chance to have as many different kinds of animals as possible for neighbors. So we loved this neighborhood of ours for being at once forested and open, hill land and bottom land, catching the sun but also always well-watered. It isn't common to find a neighborhood-sized world so various as that.

It had and has, too, two other things greatly to our purpose. There is no town close, and there are no people close;

yet it isn't one of those fastnesses so cut off and withdrawn that in no time, living in it, you must get altogether queer and inturned upon your own notions in the way of a hermit. Along the little dirt road to our nearest neighbors it's about half a mile, which, as we think of it, leaves sociability just about properly to election. The village within the township in which we are officially located lies eight or ten miles off. In another direction, five miles or so, there's a little mill village, dwindled away from a boom day back in the eighties. Over the hundred and some acres of our neighborhood, our microcosmic world in a fold of the hills on R.F.D. Number Two, there lies such a quiet of remoteness as lets us listen, undistracted, to fox yap and the *hoo-loo-looing* of the coons. Sometimes, when there is a very "low ceiling" and the wind is right, we can hear in the darkness the distant hoot of the night train passing through one of the villages. It is just enough as a reminder of every man's place as a part of humanity, but never so audible that it overlays what are, for naturalists like us, the most cherishable sounds, the primary sounds, of things: the little *squeep* of our neighbor, a tree frog, companioning us here in this sequestered patch of the earth where we have taken up our lodging with him, the tiny scrape and a bump made by the Cecropia moth that has come whisking out of our encompassing woods to cling to the window screen and stare in upon us with shining eyes.

This boundaried neighborhood of ours lies in the hill country where the Berkshires start sloping toward the Hudson River. Go a little more than a dozen miles in one direction and you are in the heights of the jagged mountains where there is still plenty of patch snow in June. Go a little more than a dozen miles the other way and you are at the edge of the mild and shining river. Occasionally, over this inland and upland neighborhood of ours, a gull comes sailing, and very often the river ducks come over. But it is a highland place, having highland climate and creatures. So it has made a good neighborhood for naturalists, this, having many kinds of variety.

If, in your childhood, you have the kind of daft and dedicated enthusiasm for the outdoors that assures you from an early age that you must give your life to this thing, sooner or later you make a discovery that proves both exciting and discouraging. You find how big this beloved world of yours is.

In the very early days of childhood, "the world" is the manageable world of the immediate. It is composed of just this dooryard to explore, from the big familiar elm in one corner to the privet hedge that delimits another boundary; or it extends, at most, just from this village to the next one, or from house to school, or from the house where you live in winter to the vacation place where you go in summer.

To Mary and me, the neatness and manageableness of the world of nature, to young naturalists of seven, are a vivid memory. The same recollection must surely come to all of us who ever were sure, once upon a time, that we were going to grow up to know all about this world.

But when you've got a bit past seven, the enormousness of the truth rushes in and overwhelms you. The world—that world you had been going to get to know all about—stretches impossibly enormous. A new picture of yourself is brought home to you as your awareness opens and expands. Here you are, in your dooryard or your bit of home woods or whatever, gazing forth as far as the horizon—and behold you are just an occupant of one tiny, tiny corner of a creation that stretches nearly limitless beyond. Walk a day's journey or a week's, and still you could scarcely have begun to set foot outside the merest parish limits, in terms of the stunning hugeness of what is truly the real world. Mary and I had thought that we were going to learn to "know all about animals," by which we meant these squirrels in the beech tree and this fox in the meadow across the way; and now the knowledge was brought to us that the world holds at least three million different species of animals. We had been going to give our hearts and lives to nature; and now it turned out that nature was vast to infinity. It is possible to "possess," in an act of comprehension and love, whatever has a size and shape and boundaries; but it has vexed and frustrated the most exaltedly mystic of the saints to try to possess, in such a gesture, the totality of things. All of a sudden, standing in our little corners of the creation, we were made to feel disturbingly tiny and incompetent; and nature had suddenly soared away, gigantesque and unattainable, into lonely space and distance.

If you must be naturalists, as Mary and I felt we must, if

you have a passionate response to woodchucks, a certain burning and heart-shaking empathy when you look up at a red-tailed hawk soaring and crying, a kind of melted-bones shivering of happiness when you hear peepers calling in the marsh-mud-smelling darkness of an April night—then what are you to do? These poignancies are lodged in intended naturalists at least as early and as deeply as the signs are said to be visited in infancy upon an intended Dalai Lama, and it is entirely out of the question to think of another destiny. It is all very well to make some money, and doubtless there may be merits and fascinations in politics or economics or sociology or the history of church architecture; but lo! it is a golden summer afternoon, and there is a veery calling in a green glen, and you must be off to follow and watch and listen, with your heart in your throat, and the devil with all other considerations. Politics? Economics? They will have to wait, for here is something much more tremendous. Here is a spotted fawn in a sun-dappled thicket, and its small pointed hoofs and its soft dark eyes are miraculous. Look, it is possible to stretch out a hand and for an almost unbearable instant feel a fawn tongue licking. Everything else will have to just go hang.

If you must be a naturalist, what way are you going to take? How are you going to get to know about animals—these three millions of them or more—how are you going to possess this outdoors of the creation? Well, there are various ways that may take you toward it.

You can become a scientist. It is the essence of science that it is devoted to sorting, weighing, measuring, and bringing pattern and order to the enormous sprawl of phenomenal confusion. In such a process there is a very real and satisfying gesture of possession, a sense of having made the unknown the known and the far the intimate. Sitting quietly in your one little parochial corner, you can contrive in a way to bring all the teeming animals of the earth under home review—you can pass them, as it were, in a managed parade under your hand—by the magically possessive gesture of knowing their names, their anatomies, their species relationships. You can know them in abstract; you can know them in *schema*.

By scientific learning you can bring the world to you. You can haul nature in from its cloudy distances to something like closeness and graspability again. But in the process you must necessarily pass from being a naturalist to being a scientist; and the two things are really not quite the same. A naturalist, pure, is a person daft over nature; a scientist, pure, is a devotee of a particular kind of strict and ordered knowledge, *scientia*. The two kinds of being are not in conflict; but they approach the world in somewhat differing moods, as do, say, a man who writes sonnets and a man who does algebra. If you are going to be a naturalist at all, you will certainly want and require to gather as much scientific knowledge as you can, and keep it as completely accurate and careful as you can, for a help toward understanding your beloved world rightly. You will come to realize early, as your life as a naturalist opens before you, that you can possess the far-flung sprawl of the world and take it to you in understanding and devotion only if you will acquire scientific learning of at least the foundational and elementary sorts of things. You must have at least this scientific grounding in First Things to take a rightly insighted look even at the sparrow on your window sill. You must have at least an accurate smatter of scientific knowledge about the general over-allness of animaldom and an acquaintance with the answers to the commonest questions about this earth's creaturely life in general.

Every naturalist must know some science, and the more, the better; but you may very well find yourself debarred, by practical or temperamental considerations or by both of them, from turning all the way from science-minded naturalist into strict scientist. You must, of course, be determined to know why that veery sings in the green glen, and how it nests, and where it migrates, and what its relation is to other birds that look like it, and things like that. You must want and seek, to this extent at least, *scientia*. But the very first thing that blazes in a young naturalist is simply love: love of the green places, love of this warm, softly feathered little body of this bird, love of the whole sunny lilt of livingness, and you may find that, though wanting to pursue and assimilate all you possibly can of *scientia*, it is rather along the lines of this warmer mood and spirit that you want to develop your possession of the world.

It lies open to you, as a second possible means of embracing the stretching creation and taking it in, to become an explorer. You can set out, from your little parochial corner, to cover physically just as much as you possibly can of all these magical forests, seas, jungles, mountain peaks and sun-baked deserts that compose the landscape of the spinning world. You can go see for yourself the hippopotamuses lazing in their African mud wallow, the penguins diving in the icy Antarctic water, and the kangaroos wrinkling their noses and walloping each other in fantastic bouts of fisticuffs in an outback Australian sheep station. You can go whizzing and hurrying and scurrying with all your might, trying to take in everything you can before you die. It is a way to see a lot, surely. It is a way to make the life adventure a wonderfully full and rich thing and, after another fashion, a way to possess this cherished world for which we are hungry. But a life of traveling exploration, like a life of formal science, is not for every one of us. You may not have the capacity, physical or spiritual, for that everlasting jaunt; and it may occur to you, too, that with however fierce an application you go running and running, there will always be tremendous portions of nature which will still have eluded you when you sink down, panting, at the end of the last exploration. An intention to take in the world, in this physical way, must always be foredoomed to a certain frustration, for it is twenty-five thousand miles around the waist of this world, there are about fifteen thousand species of birds, certainly a million and some species of insects, and nobody among us lives much more than three- or fourscore years and ten. We have only two eyes to take in this world in all its colors and contours, only two ears for listening to bird song and fox bark and the myriad other creaturely utterances, and only the one nose with which to try catching all the smells of this infinitely scented garden. You may get to thinking about all these things; and it may strike you that trying to possess the whole world physically is an overly daunting prospect.

Is there any third choice you can make, your heart being given to this earth and its creatures, your spirit eager for possession? Well, yes. You can say to yourself something like this: I'll take to me as much of *scientia* as I can, and I'll strengthen my awareness of the over-allness of this earth with what accounts explorers give, but then what I'll do is mark out, for an earth territory I can hope really to get to know with something like intensity and intimacy, one neighborhood. The world, in whole, is too big for possessing. Perhaps I can possess it in microcosm. Rather than try to get to know birds in the sense of knowing the formal names of all bird species everywhere, their anatomies and comparative featherings and intricacies of ecology, or rather than try to get to know birds in the sense of slogging through every last distant jungle and covering every last mountain peak and ocean where birds may live, suppose I try to get to know birds in the terms of the birds of this one neighborhood, this microcosm, this Particular Place Here. Suppose I watch with a single eye—and with all my heart, and with all the contributing insights furnished me from the reports of scientists and

explorers upon the worlds they examine—just this one familiar phoebe that darts fly-catching in the one familiar sunlit
barnyard here; and suppose I do this day in and day out, and
year after year, and do it with all loving attention? What I
used to think was the world, in my childhood, was a very
small area; but was I not perhaps in a sense right? May not a
neighborhood stand for the world, and is it not in a way true
that all of the much and the many are to be found, in a man-
ner of speaking, contained in the little and the one?

You may get to thinking that way, and the more you think
the more you may find that that's the way you want to go
about being a naturalist. To be a neighborhood naturalist, if
you're of a particular sort of temperament, has its enormously
persuasive advantages. It needs science, and plenty of it; but
it means that the animals you study never recede into the cold
distance of mere abstract, mere name and date, but are continually in the closeness and warmth of fellow next door. It
means you can go exploring, all right, but with some hope of
really possessing, really taking in, the world of your explorations. The round world is large and its life very various; but
it is also true, in no merely high-flown mystical sense, that
the whole is somehow represented and reproduced in any one
of its parts. It has become a little tedious, by overfamiliarity,
to say that there is contained a universe in a drop of water; but
the thing's none the less true for having been said a good deal.
Take a circumscribed piece of the world, any piece, and the
whole world is to be discovered inside it.

It's thinking along these lines and in terms of some considerations such as these that may turn you into a neighborhood naturalist. It's these ways of thinking and feeling, at any rate, that did so in the case of the two of us who write this book.

It's time to say something about the two of us. I, Alan Devoe, began being a naturalist—in so far as any follower of this infatuated persuasion can ever be said to "begin" it—when I was a very small boy in a New Jersey town. I began officially, I suppose, with the issuance of "a piece of writing." It was called, in a stately way, simply *The Chipmunk*. This came out when I was ten, in a hand-lettered edition of one copy prepared for my grandmother, and was the fruit of my having caught and kept for several months a frisky *Tamias striatus* whom I sought to get to know with such intense neighborliness, as I well recall, that I used to get inside the large wire-mesh cage with him, doze when he dozed, play when he played, and, on occasion, share with blissful boyish disregard for hygiene some of the contents of his feeding dish. My starting with a piece of writing and my urgent concern to convey in it all I possibly could of the essential chipmunkness of a chipmunk, a fellow being loved in an intensity of empathy, and taken, as it were, for a possessable symbol of all the glory of the created earth—both these things were prophetic. For it has been my life ever since to go on issuing pieces of writing; and they have been devoted to talking, if not always about chipmunks, at any rate about muskrats or

13

woodchucks or phoebe birds or one ingredient or another of this created world over which I have gone on being daft. As writer-naturalist, all these years, I have been required to accumulate a considerable pile of science; and if you give me a minute to collect myself I can usually remember that the formal name for a black-capped chickadee is *parus atricapillus*, and that an oyster's shell closing in certain circumstances is properly to be considered a scioptic reaction, and that the earth age before the Permian was the Triassic. Also, I've done a certain small and casual amount of the traveling kind of animal investigating—having a look at some bats in Panama, getting a nodding acquaintance with storks that nest on German roof tops, prowling around Hampstead Heath in a fine fog full of chaffinches. But these things in a real way have been only contributory and incidental to heightening or widening what understanding I could bring to bear, so to speak, upon the original chipmunk of here and now. The world, for me, in the grown-up years of a larger awareness and an openness of choice, as in childhood when a fellow just doesn't know any better, has seemed to me something I could best find knowable and possessable in terms of a neighborhood; and though it is good and in fact essential for a reasonably informed naturalist to have a foundation of general all-over knowledge of animaldom as a whole, knowing animals for me has meant, especially, knowing animals in that neighborliness which involves thrusting an arm into this here-and-now hollow tree, touching this here-and-now woodchuck with an outstretched hand, having this chickadee come winter after snowy winter to perch on a proffered shoulder.

Back when I was doing my boyhood explorings of New Jersey woods and fields, collecting winter cocoons, getting up before sunrise to go on "bird walks" in the cool of the summer mornings, backtracking along fox trails in the snowy woods of March, and generally falling hopelessly in love with the creaturely world in terms of the neighborhood I knew, Mary Sheridan Berry was similarly losing her heart to the world in a neighborhood, an earth parish, of a very different and distant kind. This neighborhood of hers was the countryside of County Wicklow in Ireland. Her world was a misty green one, with Old World larks to throng the farm lands on summer days, with horses and ponies to be known and loved with the kind of intensity of neighborliness that I was bringing to bear upon my chipmunk, with foxes to be sought out in their earths and worried about by a small girl when the hunt came near. Mary Berry, after the fashion of naturalists, loved almost unbearably her corner of the creation and its creatures and was eager to take it in in the way we were talking about a while back. She listened to the singing of blackbirds in the long, soft twilights of the Irish summer evenings, and she sought after the herons in the Wicklow Hills ("unlucky," these, said the farmers) and even after she had been sent off to school in Dublin, her eye and heart were always for the gulls wheeling and crying over that city and the swans that nested on the Liffey. She knew those swan nests, every one of them; and when she would put her hand into the soft hollow of one, she was undone entirely, if you like, with the wanting to hold closer and closer, and closer still, the creatureliness of this earth, the neighbor being of all things that live.

When Mary Berry came to New York, and when I had had to leave my infatuated explorings of my boyhood neighborhood and was trying to see whether a man might possibly earn his keep in that same great city by pieces of writing, we were both of us miserable for the lack of a neighborhood.

A neighbor, the dictionary says, means literally a nigh dweller; but then the dictionary goes on to say, in a lot of subdefinitions and amplifications, that the word also carries implications of fellowship, of friendly terms, even of similarity, blood relationship, and brotherhood. Neighbors are fellow beings who are close to each other in more ways than one. All these things make "neighbor" the right word for the relationship we both wanted to have with the birds and beasts around us, and they make "neighborhood" the right word to suggest what was in our minds in settling in a microcosm. All of us, whether naturalists or not, have in us an original and, as it were, instinctive going out of our spirits toward our fellow creatures in a gesture recognizing the brotherhood of all that lives. In naturalists the recognition can be urgent and persistent. It's why knowing animals by the strict techniques of formal science alone may not be quite fulfilling for some of us, nor the hurried nod-and-pass-on knowing that global explorations may bring. You can get to know about man in one way by being an anthropologist; but there's a certain chill and distance in that sort of knowledge. Some of us will want to possess our fellow—to take in the humanness of him—by just living with him, in the intimacy of daily intercourse, as next-door neighbor. In a microcosmic world you don't have to stop at just seeing a certain animal or bird, or knowing its name, or being able to classify it. You can do what it is our kind of naturalists' essential passion to do. You can rub elbows with it.

A naturalist is incurably a naturalist, and a neighborhood naturalist perhaps especially so. How are you to get to know your world, and take it in close to you, and be a part of the creaturely brotherhood where your heart belongs if you don't have a home place in which to do this and be this? After Mary and I had met, we talked of this a great deal together; in fact we talked of little else—Mary remembering a Wicklow fox earth and a dooryard blackbird that she knew as closely as she knew her name; I remembering a *Tamias striatus* that had summed and focused the whole of animaldom for me in one blaze of intimacy as I held him in my hand; both of us finding excitedly our community of the spirit that makes neighborhood naturalists.

We'd been married a short time when we got our chance at a neighborhood. We took it; and this particular neighborhood, this earth parish, this possessable version of a creation made knowable-in-little, has been where we have lived ever since, around all the seasons of the years, with our animal neighbors.

17

Our Animal Neighbors

There are blackbirds here, to be a continuum of a blackbird that sang on a flowering thorn in a Wicklow dooryard. There are chipmunks here, to whistle and chirp on the old stone fences and to offer their tunnels for a finishing of unfinished explorations into the intimately neighborly life of a small *Tamias striatus* long ago. There are also deer, also red-furred foxes, also families of raccoons which it is possible to get to know as familiarly as you might know the man next door. In this neighborhood, or this world if you like, we have adventured together into knowing and loving and coming to understand as best we can the brotherhood of the creation around us, after our fashion.

Animal Personalities

There was a woodchuck that had made a vast burrow under a syringa that we prize. Let woodchucks abound by the dozens, if they like, in the rolling fields of this farm, and let them do what they will on its thicketed hillsides. But the small patch of lawn we retain as our own, being entitled, as we feel, to a private territory as large, proportionately, as any other animal's. So I trundled a barrow of rocks to the woodchuck's burrow and dumped them in. I tamped them tight with an ax handle. That would discourage him.

In the morning the burrow was open as usual. All the barrowload of stones had disappeared. The chuck sat at his den entrance, grooming his fur and blinking placidly in the sun.

A naturalist must not be sentimental. I gathered a basket of broken glass, carted it to the burrow, and poured that in. Again I tamped it tight. A woodchuck's paws, after all, are no match for broken glass. A few small cautionary scratches on his paws, and our tenant must go elsewhere.

The next morning the burrow was open as usual. There was no broken glass. There was no sign of disturbance. There was only the woodchuck, unscratched and placid, sitting by the mouth of the burrow and pulling up tufts of our grass.

My final effort at discouragement was on a scale so gigantic as to make me feel something of a fool. But a man does not like to be defeated by a marmot no bigger than his boot, neighbor or no neighbor. This time I broke up a whole barrow-load of old bottles.

I broke them with cunning, to make jagged butts and razory slivers. I put them into the burrow carefully—jagged butts facing inward, interstices packed with slivers and needles of glass. At least a yard of the tunnel was jammed with the dense stuff, rammed tight with the ax handle. Finally, as a last insurance, I stuffed a fat ball of barbed wire into the den's orifice, piled rocks on top of that, and then laid upon the whole concoction a flat boulder which hurt my back to lift.

As will have been guessed, the woodchuck burrow was

open the next morning. The barrowload of broken bottles was gone; the barbed wire was gone; the rocks and the large flat boulder were gone. The woodchuck, neat and unweary, was chewing off our phlox tops.

This tale, perhaps, is not spectacular. But it makes plain that the lores of a woodchuck are such as we cannot dream. A man—equipped with nimble hands bearing opposable thumbs and wearing heavy leather gloves—could scarcely have picked and clawed and felt his way through that barrier, much less removed a boulder ten times his weight. Our woodchuck, scatheless, had done all that overnight. By what cunning? With what species of singular skill, with what subtle tactile senses, with what delicate ingenuity? And why do it at all instead of just digging a new burrow exit? The question is a small and homely one. Our country neighborhood has posed to Mary and me a thousand such every time we have stepped out into it.

Everybody who has ever lived has, after a fashion, believed in the soul. Or, if you like, in the psyche. Or again, if you like, in that *anima* which is the root reason why all animated creatures are so called.

By psyche we mean, of course, the interior "I" at the center of ourselves, the "that" which is the underlying unit in all our perception and adjustment. This I that indwells us, this organizing principle at the heart of us, is an evident truth to the spontaneity of our common sense.

This is our common and immemorial faith about ourselves,

the understanding according to which, in the everyday usage and living and breathing of our actual lives (whatever our theoretical conclusions), we live and act and have our being. We are indwelt by psyche; and it is our realest reality.

But what about animals? What about the inner lives of those brother beings? What of the self or psyche indwelling the consciousness of a doe deer, peering in through the window glass and munching an unexpected nub of suet, as she stares at us (thinking our thoughts there) and thinks *her* thoughts? On a late March morning, in the time when Mary and I listen to the killdeers crying over our thawing fields, a woodchuck comes waddling up out of his burrow, after five months of the deathlike sleep of hibernation, and sits blinking at the burrow mouth, peering at the world. What does this neighbor of ours make of it? What does he think of it? How does the life experience present itself to him as perceptions are assimilated and interpreted in that small, woodchuck psyche of his? We human beings have our human consciousness. What about his woodchuck one?

There are two quick, easy answers.

The first is the childhood one, and it comes so instantly to a naturalist in boyhood or girlhood that even raising the question seems nearly foolish. Animals are people. They are selves like our own selves, that most intimate of all our given knowledges. That woodchuck is a psyche, under the fur, that answers to us. We may read the thought of that deer, reading our own. Into the chipmunk that was my pet and companion, long ago, I projected myself entirely; and it was natural to Mary, when she watched a dipper bobbing and curtsying on a boulder in a Wicklow stream, to think that it sang its *whit-whit* song for such reasons as would move *her* to sing, or that it was seeing, there in the rushing water, precisely such mermaid fancies as she herself might be entertaining.

That is one way of feeling about animal selves, the childhood way, the fairy-tale way.

The second way can be readily summed in the intransigent viewpoint of the church, which insists that animals are not merely very unlike ourselves, being under the dominance of instinct and the sensory, but in fact are so altogether alien and inferior that they have no souls at all.

Where is the truth of the thing? It probably lies, as truth has a way of doing, about in the middle.

What gives to our human consciousness that peculiar extension outside space and time, that lift into abstraction and, as it were, beyond mortality which makes us speak of soul, is, of course, its attainment to self-consciousness. We perceive ourself *as* self; we can, so to speak, stand aside from the "now" of us and watch us, in awareness and in judgment.

My chipmunk, however neighborly and even brotherly as we chomped away together at the bread crusts from his feeding dish, can never have thought to himself, "Lo, I am a chipmunk. This other large animal here with the sneakers, I take it, is a boy; and now we have dined together. I believe I will review the past events of my life and contemplate the future, with a view to reflecting whether my behaviors—as, for example, in biting that boy on the forefinger a moment ago—are as consonant as they might be with what I take to be my moral obligations in a universe which I perceive to be thus constructed." A chipmunk does not reflect like that. Severely speaking, it almost surely doesn't reflect at all. Its consciousness has not risen to that self-consciousness which would let it stand aside and see itself. It has not reached that magical moment in the growth of awareness when, from knowing, it could pass to knowing that it knows—that instant of graduation from being merely an aware agent to an agent aware of its own self as significant in agency.

Very well then. So be it. Let it be admitted that the church is right enough in its traditional wisdom. No soul for our animal neighbors. I agreed to it long ago, and Mary did too—if a little more reluctantly and less wholeheartedly, for it has always been my part, as half of a naturalist pair, to try to keep remembering and urging the *scientia* part of things, and Mary's to keep continually quick and warm the felt part, the blood sympathy part, which is no less essential to right knowing, let Latin names fall where they will or be forgotten completely; and this way we have struck our balance. At any rate, it's reasonable enough—compellingly reasonable—that what a theologian means by our human soul is an entity of psychic reality that simply cannot come into being except where consciousness attains to self-consciousness, for it is only there, in the nicest sense, that self *is*.

But do we have to say, then, that the spontaneous fellow feeling with which a child or a primitive man responds to an animal has no basis of truth in it? Was my chipmunk not a person at all because he fell short of the intellect for reflection? If the dippers and foxes of Wicklow were not pondering upon themselves and the nature of being in the fashion of so many professors of criteriology at Stonyhurst, were they therefore not comrade personalities of Mary's at all as she thought they were? No, that won't do either. It's too simple.

Short of that full and final development of consciousness which is the point where human rationality and responsibility begin, there is place for personality in plenty. A being needn't know it *is* a being, it needn't have come to self-awareness or to the performance of rational abstractions to possess hosts of knowings of a lesser sort and to entertain awarenesses below that level. Mary and I, loving our animal neighbors with all our hearts and cherishing them over the years, yet agree it's essential to keep always in mind the recognition that these personalities are separated from humanness by their lack of the final convolution of consciousness whereby self comes to realize self and to meditate and elaborately conceptualize; but we also think it essential to remember that personality can be a very full and rich thing, a very close and comradely and like-to-ourselves thing, in all the vast area of being that lies below that topmost point of psychic development.

Emotion lies below it. Percipience lies below it. Sensory correlations, and in a true sense learnings, can occur in a neigh-

25

bor who has never drawn anywhere near that psychic threshold. Animal personality has an infinity of gradations, from what glimmers in the lowliest organism, squirming in a spoonful of brook mud, to what looks out, alert and knowledgeable, from the dark eyes of a deer. At its humblest, animal mind is scarcely mind at all; it appears meshed altogether in the murk of matter. But then, where it rises, it can rise to learnings and to knowings, animalwise, that make the personalities of our neighbors vivid, very near to humanness, and frequently (for there is no plumbing entirely the psyche of any living thing) incalculably surprising. The souls of our animal neighbors may be so short of full soul formation that, at death, a mouse or a starling can scarcely enter into that eternal persistence of spirit that the theologians talk about; but right here, now, in this woods, in these fields, in the earthly hour of its life adventure, an animal can be a personality of lively gifts and graces and of such lores and knowings as in their own animal way can be an astonishment.

There was that white-footed mouse.

White-foot is the little tawny-backed deer mouse that is one of our commonest mammals here. White-foot, in the winter, frequently makes his way into the deep, earth-floored cellar of our old farmhouse. By midwinter the mice have often lost much of their shyness. Mary and I can watch a White-foot sitting on one of the cellar storage shelves preening his whiskers.

We were watching one, on a day a few winters back, as he

investigated some jars and jugs and boxes of nails and the like. Presently he came upon a small, loosely stoppered jug of very old molasses. (Why this had been preserved need not be explained; it has to do with our making a peculiar brew with which big moths are lured on summer nights.) A brief and expert tussle with the cork fetched it loose for White-foot. He peered, he sniffed, he was delighted. A mouse cannot reach far enough down inside a jug neck to get at the contents. No. But he has his methods. White-foot mounted the jug neck, inserted the tip of his tail into it, and sat down. Rising, he hauled up a tailful of molasses as efficiently as a man hauling a bucket up out of a well.

That's personality, if you like—White-foot personality, mouse personality. Not much of a one, it would seem, for abstracting concepts from percepts, but finely accomplished in his own mouselike kind of abstractings.

I think of a buck deer in hunting season three autumns ago. We had heard shots across the mountain and then presently shouts and callings; and we stood still in a small clearing, surmising that a buck was being hunted and hoping to have a look at him should he come over the line onto the protected land of our private neighborhood. We had our look.

He was a small buck and had just been trivially grazed in the shoulder, but he was winded and heaving and thoroughly done up when he burst lumberingly right into the clearing where we stood. He came out of the woods perhaps thirty feet from us. We looked at one another. Over the hill the din of shouting was loud in the ears of all three of us.

Slowly but unhesitatingly the panting buck walked toward us. He came closer, closer, until he was so near to my side that I could touch him. Very gradually and gently I raised my hand. I laid it on the buck's heaving shoulder. I could feel him shudder and tremble for an instant at the touch, but then he grew quiet and relaxed. He was safe.

We stood like that for what I suppose was in fact only two or three minutes, though it seemed longer, and then the buck glanced at me, gave a kind of little preliminary start, and then went bounding away across the clearing and into the woods on the other side and out of our ken forever.

What are all the knowings and feelings and animal awarenesses that are going on inside the secret being of a deer? There's no telling. Back in our childhood we think he's a Person; and then later our church and our science (which have a way of turning out to be remarkably in agreement on many a thing, for all the notion of a necessary dispute between them) let us hear about Instinct and about the difference between the merely practical intelligence of an *anima sensitiva* and the insightedly reasoning, reflective intellect of an *anima rationalis,* and we adjust our opinion; and then finally, in the long, long run, what do we decide? I can say what Mary and I have decided, knowing our woods neighbors so long: it's a good thing to keep remembering how little we know and always to be ready for surprises.

28

Birds are not people, of course. Or are they?

No one but an incorrigibly anthropomorphic sentimentalist, it's agreed, can suppose that the consciousness of a starling is just like the consciousness of a man, or that human ideas and concepts occur in it.

It is common to the idiom of many primitive peoples to call animals and birds by some such name as the "children of nature." That term has a good deal of scientific exactness as well as the charm of naïveté. For birds and animals are "people" in something of the way that little children are. A three-year-old is not a deliberative logician; and neither is a woodchuck. A youngster does not have a clear understanding that he is a self, nor accurately understand the causal relationship of things, nor have the gift of looking into the future and into the past and seeing himself caught up in a world of time. Nor does a fox or a crow have such endowments. They are things that come later, with the "top head" of human maturity. But foxes and crows and human youngsters have in common the spontaneities of living. They share the immediacies of glee, excitement, anger, love, and response to all urgings of the moment. They share a kind of sensory-motor insight which is an earlier thing than analytical understanding.

Animals are not people, no. Not if we mean the reflective and self-conscious people of maturity. But John Burroughs, who used to have his neighborhood across the Hudson from this one of Mary's and mine, put it well and fairly when he said that they are our childhood come back to us.

It was on a midsummer afternoon that Mary and I watched the childish spontaneity of a pair of starlings at work.

The starlings had nested in a hollow in a dead maple. We had been disturbed, when they first came, lest they might molest the other nesting birds of the vicinity. But they made no trouble, none at all. Having found immediately a nest site to their liking, they had settled in it and made no move whatever to bother any of the neighboring birds. Robins had a nest with five eggs on the cornice outside my study window. Two nests of phoebes were thriving in the barn. A family of indigo buntings prospered in the blackberry tangle. Quietly and amiably the starlings were integrated in all this.

Until this summer day. . . .

It was a windy day, and we were watching the tossing of the trees. Abruptly—crack!—the old dead maple tree where the starlings lived snapped at its base and toppled. When it struck the ground, it broke in fragments. Five starling fledglings were spilled out on the earth and were killed.

The two parent starlings huddled for a moment on a piece of the splintered trunk, dazed by the catastrophe. They began a cackling and clattering of shock.

Then, apparently simultaneously, they took to the air. Straight as arrows, they flew together to the cornice outside my window where we watched. Shouting and scrabbling, in a frenzy of emotional release, they pitched all the eggs out of the robins' nest there, tore the nest into tiny pieces, and hurled the whole thing to the ground.

Mostly about Woodchucks

For about eight months of the year, when the rising sun comes up over our ancient farmhouse and lights the fields and woods of our neighborhood for a new day, the first neighbor it touches is likely to be a woodchuck. When I get out of bed and take my daily preliminary look from the south windows across the pasture, and from the east window across the wooded glen and up into the sloping field that rises there, I may not commonly see any such memorable thing (as I once did) as a belated lynx making its catfooted return toward the high hemlock woods which ordinarily it seldom leaves except under darkness, or (as on another sunrise occasion) a great white Arctic owl sitting on a post of the weathered chestnut fence and sweeping our neighborhood with the gleaming yellow eyes that are accustomed to sweep the northern tundra. Those are the extraordinary and exceptional things, the ones that get put down in the notebook. But it is a rare morning when, taking this first look out into the magically relit world of the outdoors, I don't see immediately at least one of our animal neighbors: a woodchuck.

Woodchucks so companion Mary and me, so intermix themselves into the whole texture of our outdoors-exploring days that, if John Burroughs hadn't used "Woodchuck Lodge" as a name for one of his animal observatories, we might very well use it for ours. In one upland part of our pasture, near the birch copse, woodchucks have made so many burrows that the land looks almost like one of those "villages" that prairie dogs establish. Old Dan and Frolic, the venerable horses now placidly living out their sunset summers in this pasture, often stand drowsing while woodchucks browse and scamper around their legs in troops. In theory, the whole green pasture belongs to Frolic and Dan and to six Jersey heifers. In fact, it pretty much belongs to *Marmota monax,* the woodchuck, his hordes and hundreds.

Woodchucks are oversized members of the broad zoological tribe of squirrels. But they are so very big—weighing anywhere up to fifteen pounds or better—and often so chunky-bodied, grizzly furred, and "wild animal" in look—that they are sometimes mistaken by casual country visitors for anything from a beaver to a small bear. Like a good many other animals, when you've come to know them intimately in their living variety, they prove hard to describe; for a "typical" woodchuck is only textbook typical, and the actual wood-chucks of a neighborhood vary enormously. A woodchuck is theoretically "brownish." But the old fellow that has a bur-row starting under the stone fence beside our brook is as silvery gray as aspen bark. Several of the inhabitants of the woodchuck "village" up by the birch copse are mostly fox-tawny; and when they sit up straight on their hindquarters, woodchuck-fashion, to look out over the pasture on a summer evening, the glow of the slanting sun on them makes them sometimes look almost as ruddy as red squirrels. Albino and part-albino woodchucks turn up every now and then; and many a chuck not strictly in this class has white specklings and streakings. There are also melanistic woodchucks—al-most black ones. Woodchucks are as common and familiar an animal as any home-acre naturalist can know; but it turns out, when the knowing is long and intimate enough, that even these homeliest country neighbors of every day present an endless variety and their lives an endless supply of surprising things to be learned.

Once upon a time, naturalists agree, woodchucks must have been forest animals. After all, there were no meadows, pastures, and gardens in the land before the first settlers came. Today, "typically," woodchucks are animals of the open field. The big, rufous-grizzled, lumbering Great-Uncle-to-Squirrels is habitually seen (at least by eyes that watch him only casually) browsing and nibbling in the open land, sitting beside the earth mound at his burrow mouth in a clearing, disappearing down the hole with a squealing whistle when the cows come galumphing too close or the tractor approaches. Even nowadays, however, woodchuck discloses himself to daily neighbor-watching as considerably more a forester than he first seems.

Behind our house an old wood road climbs the hill. It goes beside the glen or ravine I spoke about a while ago and it leads through maple woods, hemlock woods, and at last to the hill's open summit which is a birch-thicketed place where the deer are fond of bedding. I have been going up this old trail through the woods almost daily for many years, and Mary almost as often. We have a kind of lookout place, up where the ravine becomes very deep and great oak trees tower in a throng, and we go to sit very quietly there at sunrises, at sunsets, at midnights, at all imaginable hours and seasons to see what animal neighbors may come our way during an hour's complete quietness there in the woods. Along that old woods trail, in an interstice of the crumbling old stone fence or by the bole of a tree, there is discoverable every now and then to a sharp watch a place where the rocks or earth have been disturbed. Have a closer look at one of these places, and it turns out that there is some freshly thrown earth mixed in with the forest leaf mold. Have a still closer look, and it turns out that here is a woodchuck hole. This is entirely a woods place, altogether different in spirit and feel from the sunny fields which we think of as woodchuck territory. Here it is woods cool, smelling of pine needles, and the voices are woods voices: the long-drawn calling of wood pewees, the *teacher! teacher!* of ovenbirds, the bubbling songs of the speckle-breasted thrushes that are haunters of the forest streamside and the dark loam. But likewise, astonishingly enough, this is a homesite for woodchucks.

There are probably few, if any, of our woodchuck neighbors that live out their whole lives in the woods. Every woods burrow I have investigated has turned out to be connected with tunnelings that lead to other holes in the open fields where woodchucks customarily live. The woods burrows seem to have three functions. They are often the woodchuck's wintering place during the long sleep of hibernation. In the very early days of spring-thaw time, in February and March, when Mary and I go slogging up the wood road to look for signs of the season, we find where woodchucks have dug their way out of these forest burrows. We can never find any trace of a springtime digout at all around many of the burrows in the adjoining fields; so it looks certain that some of our chucks use the woods part of their network of interconnecting tunnels for winter hide-outs. Woods holes are also important as escape devices. Even in a field, a woodchuck can generally escape nearly any enemy, except a wise old farm dog, by plunging down a bolt hole in one corner of the field and presently popping up out of a burrow mouth way over in the opposite corner; but the possession of still another burrow entrance, so far away as to be out of the sunny field altogether and concealed improbably in the lee of a mossy log in the heart of the woods, gives an immeasurable further increase in security. It is a rare dog, or a rare countryman, for that matter, who thinks to go woodchuck-hunting in the woods. Finally, a woods hole may serve a woodchuck just to fulfill a kind of ancestral need.

The great broad sweeps of change on this earth of ours are very slow and gradual. Though we human beings breathe with lungs now, and have for ages, there was a time in prehistory when our forebears breathed with gills; and gill slits persist in our fetal necks. When our dog prepares to lie down for a nap on the hearth rug, he may still go through the preparation of turning around and around, making his phantom wolf bed. Often and often Mary and I, hearing some sudden sound or stir in the still woods, have felt that hereditary prickling at the backs of our necks which doesn't "mean anything" nowadays but which, once upon a time, in a long-ago ancestor in an ancient wood, was a rising of hackles. It is only a minute or two in earth terms, after all, that woodchucks have had pasture lands and meadows to live in. It is only a few centuries ago that they were entirely of the forest. It is reasonable enough to suppose that something of forest spirit still persists in woodchuck psyche, and that the smells of dark leaf mold and pine needles are still somehow obscurely meaningful and fulfilling. A woodchuck in the woods, by the way, is a very different animal from his customary whistling and scampering self of the fields. Perhaps four or five times, over the years,

Mary and I have had the luck to see a chuck come out of his woods hole. He slips out very quietly and cautiously; and as he moves with alert woods wariness among the ferns and moss-damp stones, he has mysteriously become something as shy and stealthy as any fox or lynx. It is an odd performance to see and think about. I don't believe it's altogether a fancy to feel that a woodchuck looks and acts, on these occasions, as though in a strange and subliminal sort of way he were making a pilgrimage home.

If a woods-tiptoeing woodchuck is rarely to be met in our neighborhood, *Marmota monax* abounds in the pasture and the cleared upland fields—now become the "natural" environment for his kind—in such a numerous company, and is furthermore so evident and approachable in all his comings and goings and doings that he offers us a continual chance for adding to our supply of chucklore. There is plenty of that lore to be learned. Even the homeliest and most close-to-home sorts of animals keep reminding neighborhood naturalists like Mary and me of what Henri Fabre said, commenting on his long and patient life of insect study. "Life has unfathomable secrets. Human knowledge will be erased from the archives of the world before we possess the last word that a gnat can teach us." The last word on woodchucks lies similarly distant; which means that we can go out into the familiar fields day after day, year after year, in the delight of discovery.

The focus of woodchuck life, of course, is the burrow. The way our neighbor *Marmota* generally makes one is this:

In a soft place in the pasture earth—sometimes right in the open but very often in the protected shelter of a rock or a big root or the like—the woodchuck starts tunneling downward vigorously, pitching the earth in a heap behind him as he labors. He goes down on a slant, usually, some four or five feet, and as a rule he makes enough of a curve in this long ramp so that no observant eye, peering into the burrow mouth, can see very far along it. As an additional protective device he is likely to make a kind of hump or hummock in the tunnel floor at this point, to serve as an observation post and semi-barrier which (if an intruder gets into the burrow) he can quickly turn into a complete barrier by throwing up hasty additional earthwork on it. Now the woodchuck goes on with his tunnel, farther, deeper, down at last to below-frost depth; and here the central den chamber is scooped out. Here is where *Marmota* will lie in the dreamless nothingness of hibernation, curled up nose-to-tail in his nest of dry leaves and grasses, while the snows drift over the pasture and all the Upperworld.

The mound of dug-out earth at the entrance to a woodchuck burrow, even when the burrow has been started at the edge of a stone fence or in the lee of a boulder, is a conspicuous thing in the pasture landscape. Woodchuck so packs and tamps the earth pile—pattering back and forth over it on thousands of comings and goings, sitting on it in the summer dawns and evenings while he peers around the green world and entertains his small woodchuck contemplations—that grass can seldom get established on it. It remains a raw-earth hummock, perilously noticeable. If the woodchuck had no other opening for his burrow, the tribe of *Marmota monax* might not nearly so successfully have usurped the theoretical province of old Frolic and old Dan and the heifers, and Mary and I might not live out our summer days, as we do, to the accompaniment of such a chorus of triumphant woodchuck whistlings.

Out from the central nest chamber of the woodchuck's home, so evidently reached by a tunnel from the burrow mouth where the pile of raw earth is visible, the woodchuck makes another tunnel. This one is usually a good deal smaller in caliber than you'd expect, to judge by the wide-mouthed passage of the original digging. The woodchuck may extend it a few feet or many yards or way over to another part of the pasture. Then he slants upward and breaks through into the Upperworld with a hole just barely big enough to slip through.

Because he has made this hole from underneath, there is no telltale scattering of earth around it. When the grass has had a few days to grow its green protection, the hole is just about invisible. It affords a woodchuck his plunge hole, his bolt hole. This is where, when he senses danger, he simply disappears in a magical erasement that still sometimes leaves me bewildered in spite of all the times I have seen it. This is where a dog or a fox sees a woodchuck vanish, and accordingly goes rushing—only to be arrested in midrush toward it by a loud chirpy whistle from another direction entirely. *Marmota,* having whisked down his bolt hole, has gone scampering through the branching tunnel and come popping up out of the wide burrow mouth where the earth pile is. He sits up straight on this now, forepaws pressed to his rufous breast, and utters his whistle-squeal of victory.

A woodchuck may have more than one bolt hole to a burrow system and he may have more than just one burrow system. He may have as many as five or six. After all, digging is in his blood, his heavily clawed forefeet are ideally adapted for it, and there are not a great many pressing demands upon a woodchuck's time in the pleasant pasture world from spring to fall. He is forever digging—making a new plunge hole over here by the old apple tree, throwing up another earth mound over there near the edge of the brook, interconnecting burrow system with burrow system by a passageway between tangled roots and rocks. Mary and I are continually thinking we know every woodchuck hole in our pasture and are continually being corrected. We know all the "old" ones, of course, the main burrows that have been established for years. There is one big earth-mounded burrow, near the place where the first bloodroots bloom in spring, into which we have watched generations upon generations of mother woodchucks carrying their mouthfuls of dry leaves and grass for nest materials every April. There is another big earth-mounded burrow, near the edge of the swamp where the muskrats live, which we have watched tenanted not only by generations of woodchucks but also by foxes and by skunks. I could draw with my eyes closed a map of the old established parts of the woodchucks' burrow system. But, though we know this so well, we can't pretend to keep up to date with the week-by-week revisions. It is a rare day, on our rounds of the pastures, when Mary or I do not suddenly exclaim "Look!" and point to a fresh little earth pile or a fresh bolt hole that wasn't there the day before. One more entrance or exit, one more ramification, has been added to the interconnecting labyrinths of our woodchuck neighbors' underground.

A woodchuck's year, in our part of the world, is about eight months long. A woodchuck rouses out of his winter sleep in February or March and reenters it, comfortably stuffed with grass and clover, in October or November. Mary and I have watched the autumnal drowsing away and the springtime awakening of our woodchucks so closely for so many seasons that, for us, it is perhaps the most meaningful and best-loved aspect of all the calendar of earth events.

As August passes into September and the coolness of the nights becomes frost-touched, a woodchuck forages in the pasture and the old orchard with even bigger appetite than usual. Week by week he becomes plumper, and with the shortening of the days his scamper slows gradually to a somnolent waddle. In springtime and even in summer, a woodchuck, though naturally chunky-bodied, has a certain leanness and hardness; but now, as he munches away at the grass and plantains (and likely munches also all the corn he can find and a prodigious lot of the gnarled apples that have fallen from our old trees), he piles up a great padding of fat around his shoulders and his tawny chest and a heavy accumulation of fat in the axils of his legs. In the intervals of his munchings and nibblings, he sits blinking on his earth mound to warm himself in the slanting autumn sun that turns him all golden chestnut, or he pads heavily down the burrow mouth carrying stray bits and wisps of hay. These are to line his sleeping place far away and down below the frost.

When the temperature gets to be consistently below about 50 degrees, it is time for a woodchuck to go to sleep. (Not that temperature is the only or even the primary factor in inducing animals' hibernation. Hibernation is brought on by a combination of many factors, not all of them yet entirely understood; most naturalists agree that perhaps the most significant factor is diminishing of light.) Our woodchucks vanish from our pasture. We may still see a stray one hastily gobbling a few last morsels of nourishment near the burrow mouth, and occasionally in very mild golden autumns we have seen a chuck still active in the pasture as late as December; but commonly by the time October comes, our neighbor *Marmota* has withdrawn for good.

In the security of his nest chamber, where the temperature remains nearly constant and it is forever dark, the woodchuck lies scarcely moving. Gradually he dozes, then sleeps heavily, then in a little while slips into the deeps of hibernation. His plump furry body curls up almost into a ball, with his legs tucked in, his woodchuck hands folded inward against his chest, his body curving around until his nose and tail tip touch. He has almost retreated, as it were, into being a fetus woodchuck. The posture is the same and the life stir not much more so.

A woodchuck's body temperature in the season of normal summer activity is about 97 degrees. Now, in hibernation, it drops lower, lower, lower, until by the time the snow lies across the pasture and the woodchuck is in the depths of the almost death that visits him each year, it may be no more than 38 or 40 degrees. In summertime he probably breathes thirty or forty times a minute and much faster than that when he is excited. Now, in hibernation, his breathing has slowed until it has nearly stopped. He breathes only ten or twelve times an hour. His heartbeat is down to a twentieth of its usual rate, his pituitary inactive, his blood flowing so sluggishly that it is unevenly distributed in his curled-up furry body. The woodchuck lies in a sleep that is as deep a nonbeing as can come to any creature—a fathomless nothingness.

Tradition has it that woodchucks wake up on ground-hog day, the second of February. It is not so in our neighborhood; and yet, in a way, it can be *made* so, and Mary and I each year seek to preserve the tradition. That is, we go out on ground-hog day and look for an emerging woodchuck and we generally find him. However deep the snow or bitter cold the day, if we prowl our neighborhood long and earnestly enough we can usually find some burrow site where at least one woodchuck has been obscurely moved to wake up and scrabble the snow away and peek out for a look around. In the interests of science it is necessary to say that this is also true on the day before ground-hog day, on any day after it, and indeed on almost any day during the whole of a winter; for an occasional woodchuck may wake up and come lumbering forth on nearly any day at all—nobody knows why. But it makes a pleasant way to observe an old calendar and tradition—so we do it.

Whatever an occasional or exceptional woodchuck may do, most of the woodchucks in our neighborhood emerge from hibernation about the middle of March. The awakening of a woodchuck is not nearly so gradual a thing as his falling asleep in the fall. It may occur within an hour. He stirs in his den, uncurls, stretches, gets drowsily to his feet. Immediately his temperature begins rising toward normal (and as a matter of fact usually runs up quite a little way past normal for a while, until it levels off as his whole body economy stabilizes). His breathing quickens, his glandular system resumes normal activity, and such light of consciousness as is vouchsafed to woodchucks is relighted in the mind in the small furry skull. *Marmota monax,* wobbling and teetering only a little, comes yawning to his burrow mouth, looks out over the March pasture, and very shortly sets out to find something to eat and a mate.

The baby woodchucks of our neighborhood are usually born in April or May, some four weeks after the parents' mating, and there are commonly four or five of them in a litter.

44

We don't see them as a rule until June; for a baby woodchuck is born blind, furless and helpless, and for about a month stays in the deep security of the grass-lined nest chamber. Our baby woodchucks take their first look upon the stretching world when it is in the green luxuriance of full summer. Mary and I like to go over to a rocky promontory in the pasture and sit there quietly in the summer sun until (as it seems to animal neighbors, who are attentive only to the movements of things and don't take much notice of motionless shapes) we have "disappeared." Then, as unnoticed as if we were tree stumps, we can watch the romp of young woodchucks around us.

Woodchucks are not famously playful animals; but they turn out, when you come to know them with this sort of familiarity, to have their share of the exuberating life-delight that wells up in all the creatures of outdoors. That gladness and relish to be alive—that spontaneous yea-saying and that sure reposing, so to speak, in the buoyance of animal faith— is one of the most powerfully attractive things, I think, that a naturalist finds in animals. No dark shadows out of the ancient Celtic twilights, Mary says, can endure very long when you watch a rabbit caper under the moon, or a tag game among the squirrels in a treetop, or seven or eight fuzzy young woodchucks scampering among the tansy and vervain and tussling with one another in uproarious wrestling matches. Me, I watch a young chuck in his first explorations as he discovers with visible daft delight the taste of plant after plant that grows in this garden for his delectation, and I see him running (out of sheer loony deliriousness over the life adventure) in all sorts of fits and starts and scampering circles, and I see him presently stretch out in an ecstasy of ease for a sunbathing doze—and it is magical to find how the writer's knots in my kinked-up human psyche are undone and smoothed away. There is a strange and ancient peace, not readily to be caught in words, to which animals can restore us; and some of us who are naturalists would not trade our moments of this for anything else in the world.

(There is sometimes a confusion, I find, if I speak of the "peace" in animaldom. A few summers ago, on a golden afternoon when Mary and I were on our pasture promontory among disporting chuck youngsters, several of them, as often happens, were so entirely oblivious of us as human beings that they came feeding and playing right around our feet. Unable to resist the urge to feel one of those firm little furry bodies in my hand and take a close-up look into those bright little eyes and that comical little grizzled face, I made a sudden pounce and caught one of the babies easily. As I lifted him, struggling mightily, and had my desired look as deep into a woodchuck psyche as a man may look, he twisted his outraged little body around and sank his white incisors so effectively into a knuckle that the blood ran down my arm in rivers. Do I need to say that this has nothing at all to do with the peace I talk about, or that to the right sort of joy a slashed knuckle is an irrelevance?)

By July a woodchuck family splits up, and the youngsters go their own ways to make their own burrows. Our wood-chuck neighbors, though the fields hold such a big populace of them, are not really gregarious animals. Except in breeding season, one woodchuck to one burrow is the usual arrange-ment. I have never known more than two. By August our neighbors in the pasture have all become individuals again, and if a chased woodchuck pops down the wrong bolt hole, there is likely to ensue promptly the sound of grunting, growling, and squealing that means a woodchuck fight is taking place.

With woodchucks so continually present in our lives—their whistlings as much a part of the familiar sound of things as the rushing murmur of the brook, and glimpses into their life ways to be had on our every country errand from fetching the mail to mending the pasture fence—Mary and I have the feeling that chucks are virtually the symbolic animal of our neighborhood. The intimacy with which we have been able to know them and the kinds of things we have found out about them exemplify the sort of relation and the sort of knowing that are the special satisfaction of home-acre natural-izing.

It is good for a naturalist to know a woodchuck's place in the scientific scheme of mammalogy: the genus *Marmota* being located in the subfamily *Sciurinae* which in turn is con-tained within the family *Sciuridae* which in turn lies within the order of *Rodentia*. It is likewise undoubtedly desirable to know that woodchucks range from the Atlantic Coast to the Pacific, in one subspecific form or another, and that the very reddish chuck we meet now and then is *Marmota monax rufescens,* as distinguished from *Marmota monax preblorum* (the New England woodchuck) or *Marmota monax canadensis* (which doesn't venture much farther south than northern Wisconsin). A naturalist must be somewhat a scientist, and it is a necessary part of a sound and sufficient chucklore to be aware that in a woodchuck's jaw there is a wide diastema. (Putting it less solemnly, a woodchuck has no canine teeth, so there is a broad gap between his incisors and his molars.) Things like this need knowing if a naturalist is to pretend to any fullness in his animal information. But the things that Mary and I have particularly delighted to learn have been those facts about *Marmota* as living neighbor which he discloses only when your life and his are long enough and intimately enough intermixed.

We had known woodchucks well for years, and thought we knew them completely, before we learned that these neighbors of ours sometimes come out at night. We had kept our woodchucks' digout records for almost a dozen springs, and had charted their going-to-bed schedule for as many apple-smelling autumns, before we knew about their climbing trees. Woodchucks (as may be learned from a dictionary, along with the information that the name woodchuck is not Old English as it sounds, but comes from Algonquian Indian "wejack") are prodigious diggers of burrows. But how does our neighbor keep his burrow clean and what does he do with his droppings? The answer to that is not in the dictionary nor in most works of science. We had known woodchucks for years before it occurred to us we might dig it up. Dig it up, I mean, with a spade.

If you look at a woodchuck's paw, studying the strong toes and the negligible little thumb, it is plain that this massively clawed instrument is a digging device. It is meant for scrabbling among roots and rocks, for earth-blocking a tunnel faster than a fox can dig it out, or even on occasion (as I've told) for somehow removing the broken glass and barbed wire stuffed into a burrow by an unaccountable naturalist. But it is clearly not a climbing instrument, any more than a woodchuck's heavy lumbering body is a climber's body. Oh, a woodchuck might, no doubt, somehow scramble up into a bush or a small sapling for a look around on a spring morning; but hardly more than that. So it looks; and so most of the books have it. But on the west side of our house grows a big maple; and on an April morning Mary and I were looking out into its budding branches, watching a phoebe.

"Look!" (That was Mary. Mary is given to insisting that she is not a naturalist at all, because she so largely leaves the science part of things to me, and because the differentiation between, say, a long-billed marsh wren and a short-billed marsh wren seems to her not merely so difficult to remember but on the whole so inconsequential, as against loving the lilt of the song and responding to the marsh smell among the cattails in the summer dusk. But Mary is a naturalist all right; and it is her familiar cry of "Look!" that has opened the way to a thousand new knowings about our animal neighbors over the years; and it is to be remembered, I say, that, after all, there were once upon a time no Latin names nor even any species names for our fellow beings on this earth, but there were naturalists then nonetheless, for a naturalist is a way of the mind and the heart and the eye.) So we looked and watched a fat chuck clambering adroitly, almost daintily, among the budding maple twigs thirty feet above the earth.

It turned out that what he was doing, this fat arboreal whistle-pig, was gashing away at the bark the way a red squirrel does in the same season, making nicks from which the sweet sap would come welling out. Evidently he had been up in the treetop for a long while before Mary spotted him and had made a profusion of bark nicks. Now he was clambering from one to another to another, drinking his spring nectar.

It was impossible that he should be doing this—but he was. It was also and doubly impossible that, when he had drunk all he could hold, he should descend the great tree trunk the way he did—headfirst. Our animal neighbors, however, have the great blessing of not being able to reflect upon the difference between the possible and the impossible; so the woodchuck came down headfirst. We watched him go waddling off toward the pasture where he belonged, and I headed for the writing desk where I belong, to enter a new and astonished memorandum in the fat folder marked "Woodchuck" in my file of observation data on our animal neighbors.

Since the day when Mary and I saw our first woodchuck up a tree, we have seen a great many more in similar situations; for it is a truth familiar to naturalists that you tend to see the kinds of things you have been alerted to watch out for. Our neighbor of the fields, who turns out to be also a woods neighbor, turns out to be quite regularly a treetop neighbor too. Curiously enough, neither Mary nor I has ever seen a woodchuck take to a tree to get away from a pursuing enemy. A fleeing woodchuck has always an irresistible tug toward his burrow, his home earth, and he seems to be unable to overcome the drive of this instinct however many handy trees may offer themselves.

"Instinct," I have just said. How easily that word does trip from a naturalist's tongue or his typewriter, and how long and long the hours he spends thinking about it, and wondering, and thinking some more. A woodchuck is only one of the many animal neighbors that companion Mary and me and furnish the stuff of both our fun and our work. It won't do to be lingering too long and affectionately on woodchucks. But instinct—well, that is something that comes up in connection with all our animals.

The phenomenon of instinct in operation omnipresently catches the eye of even the most casual observer outdoors, and not only does he see instinct at work around him—guiding invisibly the woodchucks as they build a burrow, urging a turtle toward far-distant water, sending a snake inscrutably gliding in search of a mate—he feels it stir most powerfully, with the drive of aeons, in his own inmost blood. Not only is instinct mentor to wasps and woodchucks; it is our own human subbrain, prebrain, our own primal inborn life equipment. It is the intuitive lore we possess before the intellect begins imposing its conjectures and dubieties. Neighborhood naturalists like Mary and me must feel moved to consider and reconsider it. We do our thinking, as Henri Bergson said, with only a very little part of our racial past; but the deep impulsions and protoplasmic urgings of instinct are a link with the old planetary heart.

The term instinct is a spacious designation to cover all the varieties of unlearned purposeful performance. With these our world of outdoors teems in every part. It is instinctive for a red-tailed hawk to utter a squealing, screaming cry as it circles above the hemlock tops; it is instinctive for an orb-weaving spider to spin its complex silken geometry among the grass-blades; an instinctive urge in its inner animal psyche bids a raccoon seek a lair and a mate and a diet of green-skinned frogs. Until a comparatively few years ago, science was content to let instinct go without further analysis. Instinct was an intuitive faculty impossible to explore; it was "an inner infallible voice of God" (this as recently as 1867 in a zoological journal) and as little effort was made to analyze it as to analyze the mysterious "humors" which governed the body's physiology. Within recent decades, a more intensive analytical scrutiny has been brought to bear on instinct. The scrutiny has not dispelled, nor is it ever likely to, the final mystery of instinct's wellsprings and origin; nor is a naturalist less justified today in thinking of instinct, when the mood is on him, as "the sweet grave guidance of the Earth-Mother" (Blackwood's phrase) or as "genius in Paradise, before the period of self-abstraction" (which was the way Novalis chose, in the language of a poet's vision rather than a scientist's, to view the matter). Instinct must ever be an area of many mysteries and a land of shadows. But we now know more than we once did about some of its ingredients, and we have broken it up for analysis and applied a number of clarifying labels to the parts. These things have an interest for the inquiring mind, if not much assuagement for philosophers.

We know that instinct is not a single and special faculty. It is a complex, rather, of multivarious factors.

Central in it is the most stripped of all automatic behaviors, the simple reflex. The instinct of a hare or a toad or a human being to snatch its body away from the touch of flame is such a reflexive automatism: a functioning of the uncontrolled mechanism of a nerve arc. It is, so to speak, a physiological lore, a body wisdom, implicit in the organic structure. It is a kind of response that represents, in its most uncomplicated and extreme form, a very large number of the physiological behaviors that we ascribe to instinct promptings. Instincts are constituted, so to put it, of reflexes occurring in linked sequences and chains.

The sensitiveness of flesh to flame is an extreme variety of bodily awareness. Immensely subtler and more delicate are the responses to stimuli that touch off innumerable wild creatures' performances of their instinctive behavior patterns. Bodily movements away from or toward an external stimulus are labeled tropisms, and these tropisms are of a great variety of classified kinds. There are many, many of them.

When in the dusk of a summer evening our neighbor, a darting hawk moth, seeks the whitely glimmering blossoms of Mary's phlox bed, it is activated in this purposeful, unlearned behavior by a positive phototropism, a responsive urge toward the light that is only a little less simply reflexive than the jerk away from flame of a toad's clawed forefoot or a baby's hand. A negative phototropism sends the blind earthworm creeping to its dark sheltering tunnel under our doorstep at sunrise; a positive phototropism results in the sky-seeking nuptial flight that gives so stirring a poetry to the lives of bees. The phototropisms are but one tiny category of the nearly numberless kinds of similar response patterns that control our wild neighbors' lives. It is a constitutional chemotropism that draws the flies and beetles mysteriously from the upper air to where a deer lies dead in the woods; a geotropism that governs the necessary movements, each in its season, of many creatures toward and away from the earth; a hydrotropism that invincibly pulls a housefly grub toward water; a stereotropism that demands a snake insert itself in just such-and-such fashion in a rock crevice to satisfy a tactile

54

craving pattern of its scaly skin. Myriad unconscious reflexes touch off insuppressible chains of response that guide animals through their uncomprehended destinies.

It is when reflex piles upon reflex, tropisms combine with other tropisms, and the automatic behaviors mingle to make an intricate fixed pattern that the phenomenon of instinct appears in its fullness.

We see a male frog, lusting instinctively for a female, finding her as surely as though drawn by an invisible thread, now at last clasping her in a powerful embrace which is not the result of conscious passion but of a sensitizing of the inner surfaces of his forelegs, in consequence of a change of hormones in his blood, so that a gripping reflex now utterly possesses him. We see (or at any rate we may if we're the traveling kind of naturalist) a pampas fox, inexorably led to stage a death feint when he has been attacked by enemies and so ironly gripped by this necessity of his inmost fox blood that, if the feint fails to deceive, he endures being torn to pieces without making a sound or attempting to escape. Here are the migrant birds, stirred by skeins of interior impulsion which science has not yet unraveled, winging their thousand-mile routes across forests and plains and sea. Out of the most elementary reflexive actions, compounded in sequences following one another as imperatively as the seasons, can come such happenings as these.

The enormous "wisdom" of instinct is a wisdom, of course, of strict limitations. Its successful operation often is dependent, for example, upon an environment that does not change or at least that changes very slowly. As, with the passing of ages, a high mountain alters and subsides until it has become a valley or a plain, the creatures dwelling upon it undergo—infinitely slowly, generation by generation, nearly imperceptibly—an alteration in their reflexive responses, a gradual acquisition of changed instinct patterns accommodated to a lowland life. But the process is an enormously slow one, the tempo of alteration in instinctual lores proceeding in accord with the vast planetary rhythms to which they are tied as with an unseverable umbilicus. The wisdom of earth is a long, slow wisdom; it does not accommodate itself to nervous shiftings and little changes. Old earth wisdom still urges hawk moths toward the light, though they sometimes singe their wings against man-invented flames that were unknown in nature before he came. Instinct continues to urge our chased woodchuck neighbor to scurry for his burrow, for that drive has saved a legion of woodchucks over the ages; and this blood thing, nerve thing, bone-and-marrow thing is hardly to be changed or inhibited, all in a twinkling, for one chased woodchuck in one particular field just because there happen to be some elms and aspens handy.

Marmota, as far as Mary and I can tell, never climbs trees for a getaway, but only to drink sap in springtime and at other seasons just to look out over the rolling greenness of the world.

All animals that spend considerable periods in confined

quarters must deal with housekeeping problems. If you trace the green tunnels of meadow mice through the long summer grass, you can find every here and there a kind of little blind-end debouchment. These are the mice's dung-dropping receptacles, and they use them scrupulously. Or if you watch a nestful of baby birds, you may see the parents regularly carrying away their droppings so that the nest does not become fouled. Dig up nearly any woodchuck burrow carefully, and it turns out to have a pocket or cubicle where the chuck consistently deposits his excrement. From time to time he covers it over with fresh earth. When a burrow is in use a long while, the woodchuck may periodically clean it out completely, carrying out all accumulations and adding the material to the earth pile at the burrow mouth. It mixes into the soil there, and very shortly, under the influences of sun and air, is purified into nothingness. I have gone peering and poking into innumerable homes of our chuck neighbors over the years and never have found one that had any smell but the mild meadowy pungence of clover, tansy, and yarrow, and the cool underearth smell of roots and rain. Spading into the earth mounds at burrow entrances, I have often found the traces of what must have been the woodchuck droppings of many years, but all bleached out ashy-white and sun-cleaned.

A "Look!" from Mary in the middle of a moonlit summer night introduced us to the fact that our woodchuck neighbors sometimes come abroad during the dark hours, when the pasture is cool with dew. She had got out of bed for some reason or other; and neither of us ever gets out of bed without taking a long look from one of the tiny "New York State" windows that are spaced across the front of the upstairs of this old house of ours. There are always things to see, if only the moonlight glinting and shimmering in the brook, where it winds around the orchard and rushes away past the dead apple stump where bluebirds nest each year, or if only old Dan and Frolic clomping and chomping peacefully under the stars, or if only, on a winter night, the white curving sweeps of the snow across the land. There are always scents to be smelled: brook-water scents, wet tree-trunk scents, sudden gusts of the old blossoming lilacs, or emanations from the frog marsh over where the old barn used to stand. So we always go to one of the little windows, if we're roused at night, and stand there and look at the night and smell it and listen. "Look!" said Mary, this night, and I stared into the summer moonlight and could see three ghostly animals nibbling and playing in the silvered grass. They were one big woodchuck and two smaller ones, looking uncommonly like a bear family. We watched as they browsed and scampered their way over to the edge of the moon-drenched orchard, around a bend of the brook, and out of sight.

Though we have, of course, kept a sharp night watch subsequently, we have seen our woodchuck neighbors wayfaring abroad in the darkness only occasionally. Nocturnal prowling seems to be exceptional in *Marmota's* life, as are, for another

instance, those occasions when he varies his customary vegetable diet with a morsel of animal food—a cricket, June bug,
grasshopper—or those occasions when he lumbers down the
sloping brook bank, plops into the water, and swims across
to the far side as strongly and sleekly as a muskrat. I have seen
that happen two or three times. Perhaps as often, over the
years, Mary and I have known our woodchucks to do another
exceptional thing. Very rarely, usually in Maytime, a woodchuck utters a song. "Song," perhaps, is a term a little too
fanciful for the sound; at any rate it is a sound nothing like
our woodchuck's customary sharp whistle, or his squeals and
squeakings, or the grunts and growls and gratings that come
from a chuck burrow when a fight is in progress. The woodchuck "singing" we have heard has usually been uttered
underground, when a chuck lies lazing just inside his burrow
entrance, with the May sun streaming down the tunnel to
warm him and the "wild scents and subtle essences" of Maytime drifting across the pasture in a fragrance of fruiting and
flowering that must be even more intense in woodchuck nostrils than in ours. Up from the burrow comes welling a long,
low, trilling warble. It sounds something like a bird, and still
more like the throaty trills of some of the tree frogs. But no;
it is our neighbor woodchuck, with the excellence of spring
in him, and the peace of his burrow security possessing his
spirit, and the good of sun-soak and grass-smell become overpowering; and he cannot contain his animal enjoyments.

Over the years Mary and I have had to share a good many

garden crops and flowers with our woodchuck neighbors. We haven't minded. Partly, perhaps, it is because a naturalist is continually aware of the interconnections and interbalances among all the animal lives of a countryside. If there weren't so many woodchucks here, there wouldn't be so many foxes; and, again, if it weren't for the foxes, the meadow-mouse population might get out of kilter; and then too the meadow-mouse population is connected—well, there is no ecologist who can follow out all the endlessly interweaving strands of all the web of life, but a naturalist does know that the thrivingness of the whole depends on all sorts of subsidiary thrivings, even of woodchucks; and it may dispose him, being glad of all these teeming lives around him, to forgive some chewed-down bean vines. He pays them cheerily, so to speak, as the price for continuing to be able to find a bobcat in his hemlock woods or see a water thrush teetering beside the rushing brook, for it all goes together. Also, as a naturalist, I know of actively useful things that woodchucks do in furthering the general animal economy of the neighborhood. Old chuck burrows provide dens for a great many other species of animals, and in case of forest fire they often provide shelters that can make all the difference between the loss or survival of all the small animals of a countryside. A naturalist who wants to make a case for woodchucks can sit down and diagram one. But Mary and I have loved our woodchucks, to be sure, not because of anything you can diagram. We have loved them, simply enough, for just being alive with us here, and for whistling and capering under the summer sun, and for drowsing off to sleep in the smoky golden autumns. We have loved to get to know them as fellow beings of ours, fellow lives, and to share with them in intimacy the happiness of a life adventure on this particular patch of the turning planet. For naturalists, at any rate, woodchucks make good neighbors.

The Muskrat Pool

Perhaps a quarter of a mile southeast along the winding brook that rushes through our acres, there is a shaded pool overhung by a great willow. It is near the edge of the area where the brook temporarily loses itself in the diffusion of a small swamp; so all the land around this place is damp, black, and gives off the ancient marsh smell of sedges and ooze. This is the place where our earliest skunk cabbages thrust up their fleshy green spathes in spring, and this is where the cows come on the hottest summer days to stand in the willow shade and drink from this cool pool and ease their hoofs, plop-plop, in the dark muck. Mary and I call the pool the Muskrat Pool.

62

All naturalists are inveterate bestowers of names, and neighborhood naturalists perhaps particularly so. It is a gesture we instinctively make toward more intimately "possessing" this loved green earth of ours, in the way I was talking about at the beginning of this book. I can, after a fashion, possess all the world and its creatures—the far mountains and seas on the other side of the globe, the sea otters frolicking in the waters offshore from Adak in the Aleutians, and the hump-shelled armadillos jog-trotting through the sun-baked scrub oak down along the Rio Grande—by virtue of knowing them and taking them to me through a lifetime of reading, digesting scientific reports, consulting far-flung mammalogists, and all the rest of a program of scholarly study. But this is a pale possessing compared to the way I can possess something in my own dooryard. That, I can touch. That, I can make "mine" by nearly a literal embracement. And it becomes wholly mine, it is surrendered to me, I am given (as the old metaphysicians used to say) its very quiddity, if I can baptize it.

When the first man initially stepped from a cave (or came down from a tree, if you like) and beheld in the dawn of human understanding the stretching creation lying expansed before him, he had the glorious opportunity to go baptizing *everything*. It was told in my Sunday-school days, and I daresay still is, that Adam did just that. In an ecstasy of primal possession, he went about giving names. He could make everything wholly his, in this daftly happy ritual gesture, for

63

no taint of any previous name attached to anything. He could look upward and say "Your name is Sky," and it *was* Sky because he said so. He could say "You are Mountain, and you there are Owl, and you over yonder are Deer and Mouse and Lizard"; and they were. And so he went about making everything his, and possessing the pristine world in what must have been a piercing pleasure.

It is a long time since the first man; and vast lots of the things in the world have been so firmly named that now there is nothing to be done about it. We have to accept and use the names that somebody else has bestowed on things unless each of us is to talk a private language of his own and we are to have no communication with one another. When a naturalist wants to talk about the brown-furred animal with a cottony-white tail that comes nibbling and twitching its nose among his cabbages, he has no choice but to call it a rabbit. If he is a science-minded sort, in fact, he is under the even more dismal necessity of acquiescing in the name *Sylvilagus floridanus*. And all the while his "own" name for this fellow being of his, which he can never have the joy of using in a happy gesture of ritual capture, might be something more like Little Big-Ears.

Not even all the assiduous name-bestowers since Adam first prowled through the green woods, however, have been able, mercifully, to affix tags to everything. Countries have their names, creature species have their names, villages and townships are fixed with labels; but namers have not gone through every twenty-acre pasture saying what each hillock and chuck hole must be called, or gone tagging through every woods and established that every old stump is to be known as the Thus-and-Such Stump or the So-and-So Stump. While it is no longer open to us to be our own namers of countries or species, it is still open to us to be namers within a neighborhood. This is one of the large rewards, Mary and I think, that neighborhood naturalists have. It plays an inestimable part in deepening and intensifying that possession with which naturalists like us are hungry to take the earth to us: the same kind of hungriness for intimate taking-in that got me thoroughly bitten by that young woodchuck neighbor because I wanted to hold him close and that once got me finely drenched with skunk spray—for lo! it turns out that our striped, plumy-tailed neighbor *isn't* always powerless to loose his sulphide if you carry your intimacy with him to the indignity of picking him up by the tail—and that once got me deplorably infested with tiny red bird mites because I had insisted on thrusting my arm up to the shoulder into a flicker hole, to feel under my hand the gentle warmth of the five pinkish-white eggs nestled in the bottom of the hollow. The delight of naming goes with all this.

Up on the top of our wooded hill there is an enormous boulder, probably fifteen feet high and as many across, with ferns growing all down one side of it in the rain runnels. We call that Owl Rock. There is a cavity in the great boulder's south face, and in this a screech owl once nested and raised her speckled white owlets. At the woods edge, just beyond the southeast upland of the pasture, there stands the Pileated Tree, taking its name from the great woodpeckers that hammered out their home in it some seasons ago. Elsewhere in our neighborhood there are Crow Hemlock and The Turtle Track, Blacksnake Ledge, Skunk Stump, Fox Crossing, and many another. These names will never go on any map. But they are nonetheless the "real" names while Mary and I continue alive here in the company of our animal neighbors; and by them we can act out, in a way that means a lot to us, old Adam's kind of ritual seizure of the things which he saw and which he loved.

Muskrat Pool is not the only place in our brook where we have met muskrats, nor are there always muskrats living there. But it was the first place where we found a muskrat "lodge," providing a center and focus for our muskrat-watching; and before that it was where, on a winter morning, I had a muskrat meeting that was peculiarly meaningful to me.

On this morning the pastures were white with frost, the earth hard with its winter hardness. When I set out across the fields the frozen stubble creaked and crunched under my boots, and my breath made a smoky cloud in the still and bitter air. A wintry morning, for fair, and for most of us a winter in the heart. It had been a terrible thing to hear the radio this morning: More peoples of the earth caught up in war, more children starving, more men gone down to death before the dive bombers and the rushing tanks. Another day come with no peace anywhere for any of us. It becomes very easy, in such monstrous days of wrath, to lose even that aboriginal faith which is anterior to all particular sectarianisms: our fundamental natural faith, only a self-conscious step or two removed from primal "animal faith," that the universe is somehow a good glad place and that our human kind is alienated only by its dark and crooked will.

In the wintry stillness, through the dim, early morning light of this leaden day, I walked slowly and even somberly. Almost it was possible to feel that perhaps those bleak philosophers are right who would persuade us that war is no strange and special thing, uniquely product of our human mistakes, but only a manifestation of a tendency that pervades all nature's marrow and therefore pervades ourselves who are but a part of nature. Almost it was possible, this morning, to forget entirely the scrupulous scientific demonstrations of men like Allee, and their establishment, upon a biological basis of laboratory experiment, of the ancient truth which in a less distracted day our hearts had known intuitively: that war is not a natural pattern, not a part of nature's primordial tissue, but a device of our poor humanity. Even for a naturalist, who is perforce at least in part a scientist, laboratory truths, textbook truths are easy to forget in a mood like mine this morning. I had heard the radio and read the newspaper, and these had wrought a dark, comprehensive despair not to be dispelled by recollecting the precise phrasings, the neat chains of logic by which such a demonstrator as M. F. Ashley Montague has argued his scientist's assurance that war does not exist in nature, and that that kind of woe is of our special and unprecedented devising. When a man is lost in despairing, a paper sophism will not pull him out of it. This morning, in the dimly brightening hour of the wintry sunrise, no persuasion of the scientist part of me could bring assurance that our earth has not a misery in the inmost texture of it, and our universe an unpeace at its natural heart.

The brook rushed and tinkled icily, the frozen grasses on the banks of it whispering their brittle winter sound. I made my way to the big willow, near the bend in the brook where the current rushes and swirls among boulders that are patterned by the numberless pebbly cases of caddis worms, and I sat down on the stump and stared at the dark, tumbling water. I stared a long while at it, my thoughts lost in the black speculations that throng a mind when it starts from a miserable mood and then runs idling; and suddenly I noticed, out of the corner of an eye, a little movement of a form amongst the current patterns of the water. It was a muskrat, swimming.

With his small sleek head just above the icy water, the muskrat came paddling upstream toward me. Within a moment or two after I had first seen him, a dozen yards away, he was abreast of me; and now, almost at my feet, he swerved his course and clambered, dripping, upon a boulder that I might have touched with my outstretched hand. He sat close beside me now, in the glimmering winter daybreak, and looked at me gravely, unfrightenedly, companionably, and began the preening of his dark, drenched fur.

We sat a long time together, the muskrat and I, and it would be hard to say what thoughts and half-thoughts were born in my mind out of our shared dawn-watching. I thought of the muskrat's life history, perhaps: the way of his birth, in the dark bank burrow, and of his moonlit glidings and divings and fraternizings with his fellows in the secret rush-bordered pools of our creek, and of his browsings among the wet earth-cool bulbs of the wild lilies. Perhaps I did not think at all, except the dim subthought that, in all the muskrat's life on our sanctuary acres, no harm had ever come to him, and that now he thus sat close beside me, no terror in his wild heart. Perhaps, simply, a mood was conveyed to me, more deeply than to the mind. There was renewed in me the ancient insight—call it a kind of prerational faith or call it "deep knowing" as some Algonquian Indians did—that let me feel once more what I had bitterly lost when I began my walk: the old, old peace of earth. Could I say, precisely, what kind of profound inner renewal came to me out of the small adventure of the companionship of a happy muskrat in this morning's bitter dawn, I could say something superbly important. But there isn't any way to get these things said, of course. You can only hint and hope.

At any rate, the Muskrat Pool has been the Muskrat Pool ever since.

Mary was born by the sea. Sea mists blew in across the Irish fields where she listened for corn crakes and larks, and these fields were damp too, of course, with the land mists that keep all Ireland the green country it is. So she has a great love of dampness in her blood and a real need for it. What she likes least are the hot, dry, cicada-droning days of our neighborhood in July and August, when the leaves droop dust-whitened; and what she loves best are our animal adventures that take us along the brook or into the damp coolness of the depths of the woods, where the pines are always breathing out their moist, balsamy exhalations and where little red salamanders peep out from the dark leaf mold among the shade of the giant ferns. Mary loves all animals with all her heart; but she feels perhaps her most delighted response of spirit to our muskrat neighbors, those whopper-sized meadow mice (which is what they look like, not what they really are zoologically, of course) that so evidently love, as she does, the earth's cool wetness and the splash and slip of flowing water.

So we go often and often to the Muskrat Pool, and we have delighted to put together the life story of this neighbor of ours in our minds. We start the story with his birth and try to think of his life adventure muskratwise.

Around him (as we envisage his beginnings) is an impenetrable warm darkness.

It is dark as only a place can be that is deep under the earth: a birthplace inside, so to speak, the womb of the planet. Here in this burrow there is such complete security and alienation from the bright clamorous Outside that there is nothing to give him any terror or uneasiness, no influence to mitigate at all his warm relaxedness and profound animal content.

When he was born, not many days ago, he was blind, for such is the birth state of many animals. But even now, when his eyes have opened, pale and staring in his hairless little head, there is no startling shock of color or form for him to see (as a baby robin may see, for instance, the glare of the sky or the patternings of wind-shaken leaves), but only a darkness hardly less intense than the prenatal dark. Color and the movement of shapes will not come yet for several weeks as an experience in our baby muskrat's life, and even when they do come he will not be perfectly at ease with them and will all his life prefer the twilight and the moonlight to the brilliance of day.

For the present now, in his birth nest, his universe is only scent and sound and a feeling of the warmth of a half-dozen other infant muskrat bodies pressing against his own and permeating the whole dark hollow of the nest chamber with their comforting mammal heat.

The scent ingredient that admixes with the warmth and the darkness is the scent of musk. It is in the baby muskrat's nostrils night and day, saturating all his life experience. From the perineal glands of his mother it has emanated to pervade every cranny of the burrow, lingering rankly along the entrance tunnel that leads to it, staining with stench the infant's total body and all his world. Stronger than the body smell of

71

any fox or weasel, the odor blends in the baby muskrat's dim consciousness with the darkness and the warmth and with the curious soft and gentle sound that ceaselessly is in his ears. This sound is a singular one for a baby animal to hear: not any land sound, like the crepitation of dry grass or the whistle of the wind in leafy branches—such sounds as our woodchuck neighbors know—but a sound of water. It is a recurrent splashing and rippling, like the sound of little waves.

The twisting, slanting entrance tunnel that leads from the dark birth nest to the Otherwhere which the infant muskrat has not yet come to know, has its far mouth below the water level of our quiet brook.

The sound that the baby hears is the sluicing of ripples in the tunnel's mouth, and periodically the louder water sounds that are made when his mother, gliding under water to the tunnel's mouth, enters with dripping fur to make her way to the nest chamber and proffer her milky dugs.

Darkness and water, the smell of musk and the fainter, subtler smell of sedge roots and damp, green, growing things that clings to his mother's muzzle—these are our infant muskrat's awareness of his universe and the cherished solaces around which all his life will be patterned.

The baby muskrat's fur grows quickly. The tiny, pink body of infancy is metamorphosed, before many weeks have passed, into a body very like a miniature of his mother's. It would not be well if a muskrat's babyhood were protracted like the infancy, for instance, of a baby skunk in its convoluted root-lined burrow underneath the meadow grass. For the time of babyhood in muskrat life is a time of incessant danger. The birth nest in the brook bank, with its connecting tunnel to the water, is not a safe place for the tiny and defenseless.

In the waters by the tunnel mouth, among the brook cress and the lily pads, pickerel may lurk. In the nighttime there may be prowling mink, sinuous enough and hungry enough to come creeping on stealthy feet along the tunnel. A fox, hunting our brook course for frogs, may find the muskrat den and set to digging.

And so, at an age when a baby skunk is still only a slumbrous infant, our young muskrat has been weaned from his mother's pungent milk to lily bulbs and the roots of grasses, having learned the lore of holding them in his forepaws as he nibbles them, and he has grown a thick pelage of waterproof underfur and long, coarse, outer guard-hairs. The laterally-flattened, muscular tail which will serve as his underwater rudder has grown to be six or seven inches long. He is ready to participate in muskrat adulthood. He is ready in some quiet dusk or moonlight now, in obedience to inner impulse, to move on his broad, swimming-adapted feet—the hind ones even a little webbed—along the dark, downward-slanting tunnel toward the Otherworld.

When he reaches the tunnel's end and finds water lapping there, he knows no uneasiness but only a fulfillment. All his life, in the darkness, he has heard the water lap. It is his natural element, a part of his muskrathood, like the love of darkness and of damp, green, growing things and the stench of musk. Agilely, instinctively, he slips into the water and glides from the brook bank into the flowing current and the congenial darkness of the outer-world night.

It is the adult pattern of a muskrat's life, as of all our wild neighbors' lives, to search for food, to breed and beget and have a lair, to participate after his fashion in the cooperative life of his kind, and to pass the long hours (when these concerns are not demanding) in exuberant play, or in that kind of quieter earth exultance which is a sort of compound of relaxedness and dim subdreaming.

The muskrat's food-getting is no absorbing concentration, as it is, say, for a shrew or for a wintering fox. In the dusk, in the moonlight, in the dim dawn, the muskrat slips sleekly through the water, seeking and browsing. He likes the taste of nearly every kind of aquatic plant, the tender stems of the water grasses, the bulbous roots of lilies. If there are mussels available, he takes these, carrying them from the water to the shore, depositing them to dry on the creek bank until the drying forces the shells open. Every vegetation of the water and the oozy banks is food for him; any cool-skinned frog or salamander is acceptable as variation.

Leisurely and quiet is our muskrat's feeding. He builds, sometimes, out of a plaiting of twigs and cattail stalks, a little feeding raft. Ensconced on this, while the dark current flows beneath him in the moonlight, he may browse and doze and nibble by the hour, dipping the morsels in the water, raccoon-fashion, before eating them, ready to glide soundlessly into the cool concealing depths if an owl should quaver or a red fox bark.

If, as the muskrat feeds, there should be others of his kind nearby, the suddenly realized presence of owl or fox does not send him gliding to safety in silence. This neighbor of ours has no power to make an outcry—only a curious kind of little mumbling and chirruping which Mary and I have sometimes heard him utter as he goes about his preoccupations—but he is possessed by the obscure cooperative impulse which pervades the lives of all wild things. He does not glide soundlessly into the water as is his wont when solitary, but leaps upon it, flat-bellied, all four legs outstretched, with a resounding *thwack* that is as startling and sudden a sound in the darkness as the booming of a bittern. This is the muskrat way of uttering an urgent warning.

Feeding, diving, playing exultant water rigmaroles, preening and smoothing his thick oil-coated fur, drowsing among the lily pads in dreamy half-awareness—these are the happenings of our muskrat's adult-life pattern, and centrally, as persisting core of them all, is gradual preparation of the winter lodge.

From early summer or even spring, soon after the beginning of adulthood, the muskrat is concerned in making his contribution to the building of that domed island of mud and water-soaked twigs and mounded rushes which is the muskrat's wintering place. Every now and again in the darkness—and with increasing concentration as summer deepens into fall and there begin to be tiny slivers of ice on the surface of our brook's quiet pools—he slips through the water with tufts of grasses in his mouth, with little bundles of twigs and wet, withered leaves, and deposits them upon the growing heap that is slowly rising above the water's surface in a sequestered part of the channel where the current is not too strong. Before our heavy snows come, the winter lodge has grown to be a compact, rounded mass, proof against any water current except the most tumultuous spring freshet.

There is a tunnel into it at the bottom, underneath the water, and hollowed dark chambers in the dome where a muskrat can lie curled in a warm security, musk-smelling and root-smelling and murmurous with the sound of lapping water, as was the birth nest of his earliest experience.

When cold comes, the muskrat does not hibernate but only lessens his pattern of activity: swimming slowly beneath the ice now, browsing for grasses and for air bubbles to give him mammal-needed oxygen, retiring in the wintry sunrise to the dark chamber in his sheltering lodge. Restricted and withdrawn his spirit remains—his universe a gray, damp coldness, his life low-keyed in accommodation to the slow pulse of the wintering earth—until in April his blood obscurely quickens with the warmth of spring sun and he is led at last to completion of the circle of his muskrat destiny: the lying with a warm, wet-furred female of his kind, the inauguration of new muskrat generations whose allegiant hearts will be given, as his has been, to the smells of roots and musk and dripping water plants, to darkness, and to the lapping sound of flowing water.

Or so, at any rate, Mary and I read him, putting together this neighbor's story from a hundred meetings with him.

Sometimes, watching over the years, we have seen "special" happenings, to stand out from the "usual" round and pattern. The usual life of any animal, as it may be lived typically, is something a good deal less than the real life of any individual animal, in the real living. An animal's life story is thickened with all sorts of odd and special events, when you know him in long intimacy as neighbor. Once Mary (alone near our Muskrat Pool to breathe some restorative brook smell into her and take the cool brook dampness against her skin on a stifling dry August evening) saw a muskrat—she thinks—catch a minnow. The summer dusk was glimmering toward darkness, and the Muskrat Pool is a place of flickering shadows and shimmering reflections in the water, so she could not be absolutely sure that what she saw was actually a minnow being taken alive. Possibly the small fish had died earlier, and the muskrat had just found it floating belly-up among the reeds by the bank. But at any rate the muskrat did suddenly scoop into the dark water and come up with a fish and eat it. This is altogether outside the usual life way of our water-sleek neighbor as we have known him; and Mary was as excited as ever a more formal naturalist could be to discover a new species of muskrat entirely. Another time, after we had had years of muskrat intimacy, I was watching a muskrat going overland through tall meadow grass, taking a short cut from one part of the widely curving brook to another, and was astonished to realize suddenly that it was he who was making a kind of squeaky-whimpery noise that I had been hearing abstractedly for some minutes. He kept up this low squealy chuckling, or whatever you may call it, during the whole time he was going cross-lots. I could follow it with my ear as I followed with my eye the waving and rippling of the tall grass as he shouldered his track through it. Never before or since has one of our muskrat neighbors made a sound quite like this, an entirely different sound from the mousy squealings when several muskrats are tussling together in a den or the gentle little mumbly chirrup of a muskrat preoccupied, and I have no idea what that curious commentary meant. Again there have been occasions—several of them—when Mary and I have together watched a solitary muskrat apparently, as it seems, playing a game by himself. We saw this happen one evening this last spring. It was a humid, chilly night, with peepers still calling in the marsh. We were sitting as still as we could on the brook bank, watching a muskrat make his rippling wake in the dark, cold water. Suddenly the small swimming figure turned sharply left. We both leaned forward and strained our eyes in the gathering darkness to see what had attracted him. Nothing had. The muskrat's left turn continued sharply until it became a full counterclockwise circle. And then another circle, and then another. Around and around our muskrat went, as fast as he could, in a demented whirligig. Presently, as if his turnings had burrowed a hole in the water, he sank from sight under the surface. In a few seconds his dark, sleek little head broke the water a few yards farther upstream. There, as we could just make out, he went through the same whirling-circle rigmarole all over again.

Puppies chase their tails. Rabbits in the summer moonlight play games of leapfrog and tag, and even a sharp-muzzled fox may entertain himself tossing and worrying a stick or a clump of moss. There isn't any reason, after all, why a muskrat, when the life-delight wells up in him on a spring night, shouldn't utter, in his own sort of muskrat antic, his passionate praise for the adventure of being alive.

In a brook like ours the muskrats by no means always build lodges. They more regularly make lodge structures in broader bodies of water than this one, and especially in big cattailed marshes that afford greater cover than our small marsh does. This means that a great many of our muskrats live out their whole lives here as "bank" muskrats, doing all their breeding, family-raising, and wintering in bankside dens that have one tunnel opening under the water and a second tunnel opening (dug woodchuck-fashion from below) among the grass of the brook-bordering pasture. Accordingly we can find muskrats nearly anywhere along our stream wherever the banks are right for building; and though Muskrat Pool remains the particular place where we go to find, as it were, the heart of muskrat world, muskrats are sufficiently scattered through the neighborhood to be intermixed into our daily lives almost as woodchucks are. I meet them in casual encounters as I walk the two-fifths of a mile to our mailbox, for part of the way the brook runs beside the road. Mary goes to sit on a favorite big brook boulder just over beyond the barn, and as likely as not, in the course of an afternoon, she sees a furry neighbor or two come breasting the water there. Our nearest farmer friend, whose land joins ours to the east, keeps ducks. They come paddling and quonking downstream quite often, and every now and then on some winter day they fail to make their way home and I go out to see if I can find them. Sometimes, as I scan the duck tracks in the snow by the brookside, I get a first impression that, instead of a dozen wandering ducks, there must have been a hundred. Then I get a closer look at the tracks and can make out that a great part of the mysterious duck company has been muskrats.

This neighborhood which is Mary's and my world sample is an inland neighborhood and is in hill country. But it would be a poor microcosm which did not contain representation of all that water part of animal life which is such a great, great part of it. We have it, preeminently, in our muskrats. On the hottest, dryest night of July, Mary can go to Muskrat Pool or just think about it, and be Wicklow-cool and Irish-mist-damp again. Let the cicadas drone all they like, and the katydids rasp, and the ripening corn bake in the cracked fields. We need not be parched. This stifling summertime cannot altogether overcome us with its fierce desiccations. We have our muskrat neighbors, water-sleek, brook-moss cool, their drenched fur forever smelling of sedgy ooze and the dark damp earth. We love them.

White-foot

If you have the kind of eye and ear and nose that goes with being a naturalist, and especially if you have lived long enough on one particular earth patch to know intimately all the customary daily and nightly rounds of the fellow creatures that companion you there, it is a very rare day when you can meet no animals at all.

Every naturalist early learns that any piece of outdoors has

82

a great many more animals living in it than might seem likely
to a casual glance. It is a matter of knowing how to look for
them. It is a matter, for instance, of learning how to keep
still until you "disappear" into a oneness with the trees and
rocks and the rest of the landscape, and how then to go right
on keeping still, with your eyes alert, until the owners of
keen furry ears and soft padded feet are persuaded that they
have the green world safely to themselves. The hours of keeping still that Mary and I have spent, over the years, must add
up to a total to make any busy go-getter despair. But they have
let us have a fox come so close to us that we could stretch out
a stealthy hand and touch him; and while we have sat motionless as boulders, under a midsummer moon, a rabbit has
nibbled the grass around Mary's feet and finally taken from
her fingers, all unrealizing that a human hand offered it, one
of the carrots she carries in her pockets for Frolic and Dan.
We don't count wasted any mosquito-bitten, bone-chilled,
muscle-aching minute of all the long hours we have spent in
wary quiet.

As quiet watching can disclose an otherwise unsuspected
throng of animal life in the most "empty" field or seemingly
stirless woods, so do a familiarity with the animal neighbors'
telltale signs and tokens and a knowledge of their trails and
timetables. Two or three spears of sharply chopped-off fresh
marsh grass, drifting down the brook, announce "there's a
muskrat just upstream around the bend" as unmistakably as
if the muskrat were in plain sight. Mary and I can often "see"

a fox, long before he gets to Fox Crossing where we are waiting motionless for a glimpse of him, through the eyes of the
crows and bluejays that have caught sight of him first. Their
woods hubbub on such occasions is as much a fox sign as
chopped wisps of marsh grass are a muskrat sign. Up in the
pine woods, however empty they look, a little pattering
shower of cone bits and needles informs us that our neighbor
chickaree, the red squirrel, is there with us and will come into
view if we watch long enough; and when the heifers in the
pasture all suddenly stand very still, with their necks outstretched, and stare toward the dense, dark greenery of the
bordering woods, we see with them that the landscape is not
at all the empty place it had appeared but must have some
animal neighbor aprowl along its edge—something that will
bear investigating and will likely lead us into a woods adventure.

After cultivation of the practice of sitting still and many
years' familiarity with small signs by which our animals hint
their whereabouts, it has become a rare day to find our neighborhood failing to disclose enough animals to make us happy.
Still, such days do come. Every now and then—I think any
naturalist who is daily outdoors must have noticed the same
strange thing—there comes along a day when it is as though
all animaldom, at some mysterious woods signal and field
signal we cannot detect, had vanished into withdrawal. I go
up the old wood road, and look and look, and sit turtle-quiet
on a stump while the midges hum in clouds around me in the

deep-woods stillness; and there is nothing. Mary sweeps the pastures with the binoculars, back and forth, back and forth, and would gladly settle for a good look even at one of our everlasting and omnipresent woodchucks; but this day there are no woodchucks. All our fellow beings of this countryside seem to have hidden away in burrow and tree hollow, pool-side den, and conifer top, and they won't come out.

These are the days when we take a special delight and satisfaction in the existence of a very small patter-footed neighbor whose name, to mammalogy, is *Peromyscus maniculatus,* but who is better known to Mary and me as White-foot, the deer mouse.

There is always White-foot.

He comes into our old earth-floored cellar, and runs pitter-pattering in investigation of the big oak beams, and stuffs troves of jewelweed seeds and shadberries into the old mortice notches. He comes into my summer writing place in the barn, shreds manuscripts into nest material, and makes the ink-well a depository for cherry pits. Companies of White-foot scamper in the cobwebbed air space over our woodshed. White-foot families live in the apple-tree hollows of our old orchard, and others in weathered posts of the rail fences, and others in nearly any sort of hollow-log cranny or punky-log interstice imaginable. However hidden others of our animal neighbors may sometimes be, there is always White-foot.

Our small deer-mouse neighbor is chiefly a night way-farer, with the great shining eyes, big ears, and sensitively quivering whiskers of a little animal most at home in darkness. But it is always night in our old cellar, of course, and always night underneath the sagging rough-boarded floor of my writing place in the barn; so White-foot may be scurrying and scampering in those places at any hour. If a whole day passes when he does not, it takes only a very small outdoors excursion to find White-foot at home and available for neighborly knowing. When the muskrats at Muskrat Pool determine to be withdrawn in their bankside, I can spend all the time I please trying to "talk them out"—putting my lips against the back of my hand and making the squeaky talk to which nearly all our animals will usually respond—and it avails me nothing. If a woodchuck has his woodchuck reasons for staying down in the clovery darkness of his underground, and not coming up to give an inquiring naturalist something to see and think about, I cannot persuade him. But on any day in three seasons of our year I can just go thwack one or two dead maples or hollowed apple trees and be sure that there will promptly peep out—all bright-eyed and astonished and twinkly-whiskered—the big-eared little face of White-foot. In the fourth season, winter, I need only make the rounds of a few of the birds' nests that have survived our autumn storms. I brush away the snowcap mounding an old wood-thrush nest in the lilacs or a vireo nest in a fork of the crab apple, and I gently move aside a little roofing of leaves and grasses that the nest has mysteriously acquired since last summer—and, *whisk!* here a White-foot comes darting out from the winter homestead he has adapted. White-foot is with us always, indoors and outdoors and all around. Mary and I have had a great deal of naturalists' particular and peculiar kind of happiness from this small neighboring companion.

A very little thing can touch off a vision. I remember a morning when I had been working away for hours at my desk, performing exhausting paper chores and hating it and getting more indoors-dull by the minute, when I happened to look out the window and see—framed like a picture in one pane of the glass—a tiny earth vignette.

It wasn't anything especially unusual. What the windowpane framed was simply a small section of the trunk of a big fallen elm that's been quietly decaying in the woods beside our dooryard for many years. With time and the working of the subtle beauty of decay, this tree trunk has become tinged with moss greens and earth browns, as the wood has slowly fulfilled its destiny of returning to the soil and has itself become a nourishment for new vegetations to succeed it.

On the little section of old tree trunk framed in the windowpane there was sitting, when I looked, a wild animal. Not, to be sure, a very large or spectacular wild animal, but still a wild animal. A white-footed mouse. The mouse was sitting perkily on its haunches, peering happily around the great green garden of the woods, and betimes grooming its spruce little whiskers.

That's all. The scene was nothing but that. But somehow,

isolated and framed as it was by the window frame and catching my eye in a moment when I was peculiarly receptive, this tiny nature picture struck me with a piercing poignancy and started a tumult of feeling which couldn't readily be put into words.

Here, for one second, was concentrated and focused the whole wonder and excitement of the aboriginal creation. Here was the fantastic fact of aliveness, vegetable aliveness, animal aliveness, the quivering and incalculable marvel to strike home to a man with the staggering force of a blow. Here, in small terms and humble, was the beauty of being; and here was crowded a vivid throng of suggestions—the suggestion of nature's slow rhythms of decay and succession, the suggestion of all these rhythms forming a serene melody of repose in progress, the suggestion of a kind of profound wilderness peace encompassing and resolving all small, hot frets. Here, for one instant—it is very seldom for longer—was a man, who happened to be I, looking at his native world and responding to it in such a burst of awareness and appreciation as ought, of course, to be our way of experiencing the life adventure every day.

It wasn't much of a scene I saw. Nor was this adventure in heightened awareness any adventure of a kind peculiar to me. We all have these instants.

We all have these sudden, flooding realizations. We hear the autumn geese go honking over, or we catch a sudden scent of a cattailed marsh in spring, or we see the slanting sunlight of a golden summer afternoon lying warmly across the pasture where the phoebes are calling—and all of a sudden, for a few seconds that may shake us to our depths, we see truly and know truly and take hold of an ancient unspeakable understanding. We become, in an instant's vision, old uncorrupted Adam, in the morning of the world.

This is a universal vision. It hits truck drivers and presidents of banks. It sets Chinese poets to writing poems about the Tao, and classical dreamers to dreaming of Pan and Arcady, and Christian thinkers to brooding upon the garden freshness of Eden and the bitter tragedies of self-will that exile us. No two of us human beings, though we are created equal, are created quite alike. But under all this diversity there is a unity among us, and it is the unity of a common vision. Call it Adam and Eden. Call it Arcady and Pan. Call it the treasure of childhood. Call it the kingdom of heaven. It is all the same dream, the same longing, the same ideal and vision. It's the vision of the fresh unspoiled wilderness wonder of the world, and of our fresh unspoiled self responding to it in love and creaturely felicity.

Down South, I have heard, there's a grand old phrase for these magical instants when the universal vision suddenly blazes in upon a man. They say that he's "got a glory." I suppose it is entrancement over these minutes of getting a glory, really, that keeps naturalists like Mary and me being naturalists. At any rate, these are the times of splendor. They can sometimes come, sudden and unexpected, from a very little thing. They can arrive, when everything is somehow just right for it, even with a peculiar glimpse of our little neighbor White-foot, sitting on a mossy old fallen elm trunk and attending to his whiskers.

If White-foot cannot always provide us with a glory (for that, after all, has to come from the man, not the mouse), he can and does at least provide us on any day we please with opportunities to look into his natural history and to peer intimately into the texture of his little life and so take it to us and possess it. Mary and I, being neighborhood naturalists, gladly settle for that.

Two of our most intimate neighborly knowings of White-foot have come about in our house. One of them I have already told about: the time when we watched a White-foot, in the dimness of our earth-cool cellar, exercising a prodigious tail technique to extract some old molasses from a narrow-mouthed jug. Our other household intimacy was more protracted, less spectacular, and a long, gentle joy to us. A White-foot, scrabbling through our walls one autumn to find good storage places and set up quarters for winter housekeeping, discovered a knothole in the wide-boarded bedroom floor. He popped up through this one October evening, while we were reading in bed; and thereafter he popped up through it every evening all that winter.

Ordinarily, when Mary and I seek to "get to be one of the family" of an animal, we have to go to where it lives, and accommodate ourselves as best we can to its particular woods terms or field terms, and so seek to be accepted. The old half-wit who said that the way to attract woodpeckers is to make a noise like a stump was saying something that a naturalist doesn't find altogether preposterous. If you want to be received into the intimacies, say, of muskrat world, you have to be careful not to make gestures much more sudden or startling than breeze-riffled water grasses make, and you must adjust muskrat-fashion to being a creature of the dusk and twilight. Deer-knowing demands deer quietness in your feet. Coon-knowing requires you to stand as still as a coon tree yourself. You can participate in the life at a fox den only so well as you practice fox terms and do not violate fox-meaningful things like leeward and windward. It has been Mary's and my continual attempt, by such accommodations, to seek to remove any human barrier standing between us and the spirits of our neighbors who go in fur; and reaching this sort of at-oneness with them has meant a tremendous lot to us. What we would have is so close a neighboring with our fellow creatures that our lives and their lives become completely parts together of our common life, under the sun and moon that are over all of us on this earth patch. Our knothole-popping White-foot let us have this sense of achieved intimacy and at-oneness in a special kind of way, as if in reverse. We had not gone out to his world, trying and wanting not to seem strange to him. Instead he had come into our world, and it had not seemed strange or alien to him at all. The bedroom, from the way he took to it, might have been only a somewhat oversized mouse hollow among the roots of a beech tree. Mary and I, in our native habitat, were nothing strange to him, but as comfortably acknowledgeable parts of the neighborhood night as might be stumps or boulders. During that winter of White-foot's nightly visits to us, we had a rare delight in his acceptance of us.

White-foot would come out of his knothole every night at eleven o'clock almost exactly. All animals observe time schedules. I could set my watch by the morning appearance of deer on the sumac-grown east ridge of our neighborhood where the sun comes up, and I could check it again by the deer's twilight browsing time in the pasture flat by the birch copse. The sense of rounds and seasons, light and dark, flower openings and flower closings—all the rhythms of earth event—is vivid and meaningful in animal life. Sometimes when Mary and I haven't looked at a watch or clock for a few hours, we take a moment and try to guess the time. After all, we have been woods-familiar and field-familiar for many years now; and the "feel" of the hour should be as available to us as to our neighbors. Still, we miss by a quarter or a half hour. A common honeybee would do better. In experiments in England, naturalists have found that when food is put out for bees at a regular hour every day, the bees soon learn to come flying in from the countryside at the feeding hour with such exact timing that their arrival seldom varies by as much as five minutes— so delicate is their expertness. Bees and ants can even be anesthetized for several hours and still adhere to the time schedule they have learned to follow. They still get to the right place at exactly the right time. Our White-foot visited our bedroom with the same scheduling with which, in his woods world, he would visit at a particular night hour the beech-tree hole, and at another particular night hour the hemlock stump, and at another hour, on his pattering rounds in the woods darkness, the old fallen hickory tree where squirrel-cached nuts might be found. He incorporated us into his White-foot world, making us part of it; and the sense of this was a melting pleasure to naturalists like Mary and me.

At eleven, our small neighbor's tiny white forepaws would appear through the knothole, holding fast to the sides of it as he prepared to swing himself up. (For informal naturalists, more concerned with the loving and intimate knowing of animals than with their classification, scientific nomenclature may often seem a nuisance. But it can turn out to have its own kind of felicity, hidden in the Greek or Latin. *Maniculatus* means "with little gloves.") Then we would see the twinkling, quivering nose, the soft, dark eyes, the alerted whiskers. Our White-foot would hoist himself clear of the knothole, and pause tentatively for a second. A White-foot has a great many enemies. Owls may glide down at him, on their soundless wings, in the darkness. Foxes watch by his runways. Snakes and weasels are sinuous enough to slip into his burrows in pursuit of him. So our White-foot would pause carefully on entrance and raise his little muzzle and sniff—this way, that way, this way, that way—and peer sharply around, in the unaccustomed brightness, to see whether there was any dangerous creature here. But no, there were only Mary and I, natural and native-seeming enough beings, evidently, to be found inhabiting a mousehole. Our White-foot would make a kind of scampering rush across the floor, invariably following the same zigzag trail he had established among these invisible leaves and grasses the night before, and then come swarming up the light cord onto the bedside table.

All mice are lovely, I think. But dully dusky little *mus musculus,* the house mouse, though originally a field dweller, for so long and in so many places has had to achieve survival as a furtive pilferer in the darkest and dirtiest crannies of city life that there attaches to him almost inseparably a suggestion of the slums. White-foot retains all his wild delicacy and woods freshness. He is a little wild animal; and what suggestions attach to him are all moss hints, fern hints, and cedar-bark suggestions. When our visitor would come scurrying up the lamp cord, as in his outdoors world he loves to scurry up wild grapevines, and would presently settle in the circle of amber lamp light on the table, Mary and I would have a chance to see, as we had never quite seen before, the small, extraordinary beauty of this forest friend of ours.

White-foot has an over-all length of perhaps seven or eight inches, from twinkling nose tip to the end of his tail, but at least three inches of this is tail. Above he is soft brown-strawy —deer color, in fact—and underneath he is a clear immaculate white. The tawniness of his upper parts and the snowiness of his underneath nowhere merge or blur where they join. They are demarked by a clear, sharp line, as firm as if drawn. This abrupt separation of his colors extends even to his tail (a much more adequately furred tail than the bare bedragglement a *mus musculus* trails). Above a clearly defined median line, White-foot's tail is dark grayish-brown; beneath, it is as white as his snowy throat, chest, stomach and paws. Around White-foot's big lustrous eyes and the base of his whiskers, the tawniness of his little pointed face is marked with a darker dappling, nearly black. Perhaps the thing Mary and I loved most to watch, in the lamp light, was our White-foot's ears. They are big, dark velvety-brown, and they are outlined with an ashy-gray edging. White-foot, when you can see him close up like this, and in bright light, has something of the color quality and pattern quality of one of the great moths that come to the summer evening garden, a Cecropia perhaps, or a Polyphemus.

During all his winter of nightly visits our White-foot never did anything spectacular. We kept hoping that perhaps some night he might sing; for these mice do sing—a thin little wiry trilling song, like finch twittering—and because of their love of darkness it is almost impossible to see them at it. (Some country people still use a good old name for White-foot. They call him a vesper mouse.) But he never did. I suppose it would have been too much to expect. What he came to Mary's and my large mouse room for, of course, were the foodstuffs of which he found this part of his burrow singularly productive;

and he addressed himself every evening to the feeding dish under the lamp. We kept it filled with crumbs of stale bread, crackers, and sunflower seeds. White-foot would sit gravely nibbling and shucking, in the circle of lamp light, for perhaps fifteen minutes; and then for nearly as long again he would clean and preen and tidy himself. He washed his face and groomed his whiskers over and over again, cat-fashion, and he would lick and smooth his soft white fronting scrupulously from as high up on his chest as he could reach right down to the root of his tail. More often than not, White-foot concluded the performance by sneezing. I don't know why there should have been something queerly touching about these sneezes of his, but there was. Perhaps it was because they were so tiny, and withal so earnest. We would see him lift his face, blink his eyes uncertainly at the lamp, and then —*ptpch!*—there would be delivered the infinitesimal explosion. White-foot would at once hurry down the lamp cord, scurry across the floor by his established zigzag woods trail, and whisk down his knothole to remain absent on other White-foot errands for the next twenty-four hours.

Our visits from White-foot stopped in April. They never resumed. Perhaps he was taken by a predatory neighbor. Perhaps he just went out to find a mate, and was so caught up in the earth's thaw-time excitements, in this season when the frogs are chorusing in our marsh and the spring night is heavy with the smell of rain-wet buds and the first thrust of growing things, that he forgot all about his winter quarters, including that large chamber, off at the end of one gallery, which had been so curiously bright and unaccountably rich in sunflower seeds.

Like all mice, White-foots are fecund. There are usually several litters a summer, and a young White-foot reaches sexual maturity and is ready to beget babies of its own when it is only about sixty days old. The first families of the season are under way, in our neighborhood, by the latter part of April at latest, the White-foot infants being born about three weeks after their parents' mating.

Because White-foot is usually so strictly nocturnal and because, even when he makes our house an extension of his woods world, we can't usually watch him in such intimacy as we enjoyed during that one winter, Mary and I have had most of our close-up glimpses into White-foot's life on occasions when we have disturbed a family in its nest.

When a White-foot nest containing mother and babies is seriously disturbed, one of two things often happens.

If the little pink mouselets are not suckling at the time, the mother White-foot may slip from the nest and withdraw into hiding a few feet or a few yards away, and then, when she thinks the danger has passed, she may come pattering back, pick up her babies one by one, and carry them off to a new, safer location. Holding ourselves in our familiar and almost automatic gesture of frozen stillness, Mary and I have often watched these rescues. The mother White-foot carries her little ones the way a cat does (or a squirrel), by the napes of their necks. She frequently has to make as many as five or six trips, and it is extraordinary to see how fast she can go scampering among the withered leaves of the woods' floor or the dusty litter in the barn loft without ever bumping one of her small pink burdens against anything or dropping it.

What happens when a White-foot household is disturbed during suckling time—and of course a baby White-foot, like any baby animal, spends a great part of its infancy in milk-drinking—provides a spectacle that I first came across (having pulled over a dead hemlock stub in a small woods near my boyhood home) when I was a naturalist of about ten. I was held spellbound, then, with astonished delight over it; and I continue feeling the same way nowadays, often as this particular mouse adventure has occurred to me since. A baby White-foot, suckling, grasps its mother's tiny mouse-milky teat with a sucking grip of prodigious firmness. Nipple conformation and the baby White-foot's little mouth conformation fit together so excellently that when the suckling reflex is in operation the youngster is all but undetachable. So what happens, when I sound my rap on the hollow tree trunk or reach my hand inside the old stump, is that the startled mother White-foot comes scurrying out with her whole brood of pink offspring unshakably fastened to her. They dangle from her snow-white underside like a cluster of so many little berries or seed pods. If my intrusion has not too seriously disturbed her, she sometimes feels sufficiently reassured, after I have "frozen" for a few minutes, to go back into the nest and let feeding resume as before in its soft, mouse-warm security. But if her misgiving persists, she may go scampering off to find a new shelter; and perforce she carries her babies with her as suspended cargo. So careful when she carries her babies in her mouth, she seems heedless of them when they hang like this, and she rushes away at a jouncing scamper, little pink infant mice scraping the ground or banging against bits of undergrowth at every step. It's seldom that one loses its grip, though; and presently the whole jiggling little caravan has disappeared to safety.

A young White-foot is weaned by the time he is three weeks old. He leaves the birth nest to take up the pattern of what will be his adult-life way looking surprisingly unlike his russet-backed little parents. An immature White-foot's upper parts are a dull brownish-gray to silvery gray, and the streak along the middle of his back is nearly black. The outsides of his ears, too, are nearly black, and the insides almost altogether white. Around the margins of his ears runs a sharply marked white edging. When I have disturbed a White-foot nest from which the youngsters were big enough to go bolting under their own power, I have sometimes been startled to see what at first glance seemed to be a scampering company of gray house mice.

Young White-foot, launched into adulthood, goes about such woods learnings as any other of our wild animal neighbors must acquire: food-finding, tracking and trailing, establishing himself in a particular "territory" of the dark countryside. I think I have been calling him a "wild animal" rather insistently in these accounts of our adventures with him. But so in fact he is; and in the combination of his wildness of woods spirit, his complete kindred to forest ways and forest things, with his being so small and so "only a mouse," lies a good deal of the special charm of him.

Take tracking, for instance. A White-foot can track like a panther.

One moonlit autumn night I had gone off up the old wood road beside the ravine. I wasn't looking, particularly, for any woods adventure; for a bright moonlit night, though it may seem to a man the pleasantest kind of night to be outdoors, does not seem so to most of our animal neighbors. They mistrust the clarity of such nights, both preyers and preyed-upon, for it makes them feel uneasily visible to watching eyes. Our neighbors of the dark hours dislike a too-clear night as they dislike a too-windy one. When the wind whips every which way through the woods, scents are confused. Mary and I have always had our most rewarding nocturnal watches outdoors on very still nights when there has been drifting, high cloudiness. I had gone up the old trail through the woods, this night, just to enjoy the autumnal outdoors, and smell the scents of withering asters and fallen yellow and scarlet maple leaves with their night freshness on them, and perhaps just sit on an old stone fence and let myself be drenched in the moonlight.

Almost all naturalists talk incurably about their philosophy. What it really comes down to a good deal of the time, I shouldn't wonder, is just our loving to be animals ourselves. We "come at our enchantments," as the stately Emerson put it, in the exercise of a psychic-sensuous relish, and repose in an in-the-bone knowing, not so very far removed from the aboriginal satisfactions of any mouse or muskrat and the un-formulated knowings that sustain them.

In a clearing among young aspens, I sat down on an old stone fence, and was thinking to myself some moon-soaked thoughts about animal faith, and sureness, and the knowledge that comes drenching in, in the woods silence and stillness.

The most famous cautionary tale for would-be philosophers, I was thinking, is perhaps the very old story about the centipede. This centipede, it will be recalled, had spent a happy lifetime pursuing the various activities of centipedehood, scurrying proficiently on its hundred legs wherever its inclinations might lead it. It was a contented centipede, active and effective. Then one day the centipede was halted on its rounds by a questioner. The questioner said: "Centipede, I am fascinated and astonished to observe how you walk around so proficiently while maneuvering no less than fifty pairs of legs. I should think it would be extremely difficult. Tell me, when you start to walk, which leg do you move first?"

Never in the entire life of the centipede—so active, so effective, so full of easy assurance—had this question ever occurred to its mind. It bent its intellect upon the question.

Which leg—come to think of it—*did* one move first, in order to start walking?

The centipede thought and thought. Leg number eight? Leg number fourteen? The centipede worked itself into an agony of analysis and indecision. And, so the story goes, the centipede was never able to walk another step. Paralyzed by its intellectual problem, it remained immobile where it had been halted, and slowly starved to death.

Akin to this distressing tale is the only slightly less celebrated one known as the story of Buridan's ass. It is supposed to have been invented by the enemies of that philosopher to ridicule his views about the operation of the will. The anecdote has it, at any rate, that a hungry ass was once placed, free of restraint, between two identically tempting bundles of hay which were exactly equidistant from it to the right and to the left. The miserable animal, since the attraction of the right-hand bundle was exactly counterbalanced by the attraction of the left-hand bundle, could (obviously) only remain motionless between the two, imprisoned in irresolution until, like the hapless centipede in the other story, it died of starvation.

These ridiculous yarns have survived for a good many centuries, and they will undoubtedly continue to do so indefinitely. For they illustrate, with a fine absurdity, the perils of a too-devoted intellection.

It is the intellect that has given humankind all its many and peculiarly human distinctions. It is only because we pos-

sess intellectuality that we are able to build much more remarkable suspension bridges than spiders can and are able
to compose music, design systems of politics and economics,
and construct complicated theories of metaphysics. Indeed,
it is only by virtue of our intellectual faculty that we are able
to look forward into the future, and to summon and scrutinize
the past, and thus escape from that time-world in which all
the other parts of nature are held forever as captives of the
immediate. The intellect is a precious and estimable tool, de-
serving all our championing and most assiduous training.

But it is in the very nature of this instrument—this faculty
which permits its user to know himself as a self, and to look
upon the whole scene of self and otherness with the kind of
questioning called rationality—that it can become a danger.
It can, that is to say, come to be so overregarded by its user
that he invests it with a sort of total authority which it does
not in fact possess. Entranced by the efficiency and agility of
his own power of thought, a man can fall into the false pride
of supposing that all truth whatsoever, to be accepted as legiti-
mate and to be acted upon, must be intellectually established.
This pride of intellect has, of course, been the immemorial
disease of philosophers, and in less drastic forms it comes along
to befuddle all of us now and then.

There results the spectacle of a philosopher writing eight
or nine volumes of exquisitely complicated reasoning in an
effort to prove, to the satisfaction of his intellect, that he exists. There result libraries full of intellectual dissertations

which seek to establish that the objective world is indeed really there, and that we really have a certain power of choice in the performance of our acts, and that it is "better" in some logically and intellectually provable way to be alive than to be dead. Occasionally there results an unhappy man whose furious intellection has brought him to the impasse and paralysis of a total inability to believe *anything*. Unable, by thought, to establish any of those necessary first principles without which no edifice of belief can be built, he can only remain as tragically motionless as the introspective centipede or the starving ass which had no logically defensible reason for choosing one bale of hay rather than the other one.

It is a salutary reflection that the overwhelmingly major part of the world of nature goes forward with no intellection at all. Foxes breed and find their food and manifestly have fun in the meadow, though it can never have occurred to any fox to try to prove, in a set of vulpine syllogisms, that he really exists and really has fur on his haunches. No bird can ever have made an intellectual inquiry into whether, logically, it is desirable to utter a song at the rising of the sun. The sun is seen and felt, and a song wells up. No coon lies dozing delightedly in a tree fork in the summer noon because he has established an unassailable demonstration that this is good. He feels it; he knows it; he acts on it.

What all animals act upon is describable, exactly enough, as animal faith. What they know, in their unself-conscious way, they know with dumb certainty.

Ourself an animal, we bring to the life experience as our primary equipment precisely the same kind of dumb certainty, the same sort of immediacy of unformulated conviction. We "know" that the world is real in the instant when our sensory-motor experience tells us that it is. We know, in the first instant of the experience of the self, that this is as compelling an awareness of the real as is our experience of the rough bark of a hemlock tree or our experience of the sound of the song of a bird. We know that it is good to play a game, and that it is good to lie down weary to sleep, and that the taste of food is a good and that the feel of the rain is a good. We know all these things, and a thousand others, before we know we know them. They are our "given"; they are what is lodged in us; as immediate a provision as what informs the spontaneous psyche of any owl or bat or fox or bird as its awareness opens to the adventure of being alive. We know these first things, so to speak, by direct apprehension of our total organism.

No platoon of furrow-browed philosophers can "prove" these primary knowings. They are animally basic; and it is not possible for the intellect to get, as it were, behind them. They are not rational things. They are not things that may be made problematical or that may be debated. They are first things. They are the sureties of animal faith. Who does not accept them does not accept the gift of life as it is given.

It may be galling to our pride, to be sure, to accept what we cannot compel to pass our proud intellectual tests. If we cannot affix the seal of our intellectual endorsement, we may be inclined to reject the offering. If we are to maintain our mental health and balance, however, the severe fact is that we have no choice.

Spiritual teachers have been saying for a good many ages that the most valuable and necessary thing in the world is probably humility. In the matter of the right use of the intellect, it is surely true. If we overexalt it, and think to give it a godlike competence and universal authority, we end by its turning upon itself and destroying the validity of its own conclusions. If we acknowledge it to be only what in truth it is—a useful faculty, but forever incompetent to penetrate to the heart of the great underlying mysteries and analyze them into terms of human comprehensibility—we can create, on the foundation of an animal faith which with humility we acknowledge to be unprovable, sound structures of intellection that are our race's lasting glory.

It is the fundamental fact of our human situation that before we can act, before we can think, we have to make an act of faith. To be wise, we have to be willing to be as simple as a woodchuck. We have to be willing not only, in Thomas Huxley's phrase, to sit down before fact like a little child; we have to be willing to be as spontaneously believing as a sleek-furred muskrat at Muskrat Pool, as animally trustful as all the other creatures of the world of nature are. Make this initial act of faith, and the intellect and will are set free to think and act. Withhold this first allegiance, withdraw our animal faith, and we are paralyzed forever in a snare of sophistries.

What is required of us is only this: that we humble ourselves to creatureliness with all the rest of the brotherhood of the earth. What is required of us is only this: that we take on faith, with trusting hands, the gift of life as it is given, and bow our heads a little.

Or so it seemed to me, in the harlequinade of the autumn moonlight, sitting on my lichened old stone fence among the aspens. The restoration of some primitive simplicities like these would have been reward enough, and rest, for a forest hike at night. But now I was given also a small animal adventure. Out from the brush at the other side of the little moonlit clearing came pattering an intent white-footed mouse. I froze to alerted immobility.

White-foot had his tiny pointed muzzle close to the earth, as though he were following a scent trail. He was going remarkably fast, and his scurry across the clearing followed a strikingly erratic course, hither, yonder, zigzag, back to straightaway again. I watched him make a last erratic run around a tussock of tall grass and disappear into the darkness of the aspen scrub.

Only an instant had passed when a second White-foot rushed at a bouncing scamper into the clearing from exactly the point where the first White-foot had entered it. This time it was unmistakable that I was seeing our small nocturnal neighbor White-foot in his role as tracker; he was on the trail of the first White-foot. I watched him go tearing along, his quivering little nose to the earth, his little white feet furiously a-patter, and saw him follow exactly every tiniest twist, turn and zigzag of the first White-foot's course. Without ever hesitating or slackening, the trail-follower made the last rushing dart around the tussock of tall grass and disappeared at full scamper into the aspen scrub on his absorbed pursuit.

The whole brief episode, under the autumn-frosty moon, could not have had more high animal excitement in it if pursuer and pursued had been beasts as big as panthers. White-foot is very little; but he is a wild animal. He can carry with him all the elemental quality of wildness and the night. He can be woods-fleet, gripped by wild urgings and exercising a wild animal's sensory acuities as he responds; he can bespeak the primal as eloquently as much bigger four-footed neighbors of ours that slip through the darkness. He is forest-hearted, this little one.

As I came down along the old trail toward home, I had had more than I had bargained for. I had thought to do some moon-soaking, and some smelling of the autumn night smells of withered leaves or hickory husks, and perhaps some of that thinking (or not thinking, if you will) by which naturalists like Mary and me, in our meditative times outdoors, are continually repersuaded to the nature faith which is so substantially animal faith and so underpins our philosophy. Fulfilled in these things, I had likewise had a new experience with one of our animal neighbors—not a great dramatic experience nor a rare neighbor. But all the same, under the moon, I had come that much closer and deeper into community with our shared lives here. I had had an adventure, and I had seen something and learned something; and if only by a little I had become a fuller and wiser knower of one neighbor.

That has always been White-foot's function, in Mary's and my life over the years of our animal adventuring together in these woods and fields of ours. He provides us, every day, any day, with an animal neighbor available, to disclose to us a new fact, to communicate to us dependably, if only in his small White-foot way, the excitement of animal things, to keep us happy with the sense of animal closeness and of ever-increase in our neighbor-knowing of the lives that companion us.

White-foot is only a mouse. But he is a lovely mouse, tawny as a deer, immaculately white, full of animal lores of his special White-foot kind and practitioner of ways that re-ward learning. Intimate in our lives with a constancy and closeness no other animal neighbor of ours can very well have, this little storer of jewelweed seeds in our cellar and wild cherry pits in my inkwell has seemed to Mary and me, in his White-foot way, to have his inestimable merits.

Discovering the Deer

In my boyhood there was a popular kind of writer-naturalist who never seemed to visit the woods or go tramping across the fields without coming upon some vividly dramatic episode of animal life.

One of these men would step into an evergreen grove and in an instant would discover that he had happened upon an extraordinary "school" being conducted by the crows in those green depths. In the space of a few minutes he would be able to observe the elder crows instructing the young ones—

putting them through wing drills, chastening them for faults and disobediences—and he would see easily a dozen astonishing crow happenings worth remembering and recording. Such a writer-naturalist as this never seemed to scan the tree-tops and see only, say, a gray squirrel nibbling an acorn, or study the pastures stretching warm in the summer sun and see only, say, a woodchuck bending down the tall weed tops with its forepaws to get at the budding blossoms. What he would see, looking up, would be a hugely exciting battle between the gray squirrel and a great horned owl that had chanced to choose the same tree for midday dozing. What he would see, looking out over the summery acres of tansy, vervain, and mullein, would be a desperately dramatic encounter between a woodchuck youngster and a big blacksnake; and this would disclose to him enough remarkable woodchuck ways and snake ways to make at least a full chapter of a breath-takingly engrossing book.

Not only did these literary outdoorsmen of my boyhood see startlingly dramatic episodes of animal life nearly every time they went out along a woods trail; they were also able to have individual animals so continually under their eye that they could follow the whole life course of an animal, in daily and almost hourly observation, from the moment of its birth until the time when it met its memorable death in the final superb struggle, perhaps, with a giant white-headed eagle. An animal, so to speak, stayed *handy* for these naturalists. It remained available, so that its life story unrolled before the watcher's eye as a continuous narrative, and did not have to be pieced together, over years of watching many different individuals, from bits and fragments and momentary glimpses vouchsafed.

An incomparable help was provided by the way so many individual animals turned out to have peculiar distinguishing marks or characteristics. The woodchuck whose life from birth to death was being watched and recorded was early discovered to have an unusual splash of white fur on its rufous breast; and this not only made it possible readily to single out this particular woodchuck from all the other grizzle-furred chucks scampering in the clover, but, in writing about this woodchuck, to call him Silverpatch. As Silverpatch went through the rounds of his days, under the never-absent eye of the naturalist who was their historian, the other animals he encountered—in dramatic battles, contests of woods stratagem, and so on—were as likely as not also similarly identifiable. Silverpatch would be chased to his burrow not just by a red fox but by the particular and peculiar red fox who had years ago lost a forefoot in a trap and who thus had a special identity as Old Peg Leg. It was not just "crows" that sometimes swooped down on Silverpatch in the meadow, to tease him with raucous corvine antics of the sort Mary and I watch in our fields, but a band of crows under the leadership of the particular crow, Feather Flag, one of whose tail feathers had an unmistakable sidewise slant that gave him a unique banner of personality.

I should not wish to make fun of those magical old books of my boyhood, beyond the gentlest. Reading them, I was made authentically to feel the spell of animal life. The woods and fields, to which my heart was already given, were invested with increased excitement and made to hold out such possibilities of adventure as a naturalist's dreams are made of. The writers of these old nature books often really had the "feel" of animals—and the feel of the green woods depths, the sunny fields, the shadowy brook pool where at dusk the white-tailed deer stand drinking—with a vividness and passion; and they communicated this. It is no small thing to do. If they were men whose imagination made them populate the outdoors with such an abundance of wild creatures as less dream-haunted investigators could not discover and if they pretended to themselves to have followed Silverpatch and Feather Flag with a firsthand hourly intimacy, and through dramatic adventures, hardly possible except in the realm of the mind's fancy—well, it was only because they were men of this imaginative power that they were also able to ensorcerize a reader with the very breathing woodchuckness of Silverpatch, the very crowness of Feather Flag, and the very pondscum smell, cool reediness, and midge-cloud dance of the quiet pool in the dusk. They paid a certain price in precision for their power; but the power was real and great, and sometimes let them achieve, at their best, a largeness of essential truth that transcends exactness of particularities.

I used to take their books into hideaways in my boyhood

woods and read them by the hour, spellbound. Mary used to read them in her Irish girlhood, with the same quickening of spirit. If the foxes to be found in the green Wicklow coverts were not quite so continually available as the ones in the woods she read about, and if there seemed seldom to turn up a distinguishable Peg Leg among them or be observable a battle to the death between Peg Leg and a screaming falcon, still the woods-devoted heart of a small girl was all the more confirmed in its naturalist's bewitchment and an already sharp pair of watching eyes was made all the more eager and alert. Neither Mary nor I can smile too wide a smile, nor in any mood but an affectionate remembering, over those old books.

However, it has to be acknowledged that the woods of our own neighborhood, which have been the world we have intensively explored in daily intimacy over our years together, are not like the woods we read about in childhood. Our animal neighbors, the most intimate possible knowing of whose lives and selves has been our work and delight, do not turn out, in firsthand intimacy, to be either so easy to watch or so abundant in easily distinguishable individuals as some of the old literary naturalists seemed to find them. Our familiar crows here do many delightful things: building their bulky stick nests up along the wood road, sailing down the blustery October wind, flapping silently to their winter roost against the leaden, streaky sky of December afternoons. But though I have spent a great many thousands of hours in crow company, and have "talked" with them and shinnied up to their nests and watched them from hiding in all seasons, I have not found them conducting a school.*

All this has to be acknowledged. A great many people were brought up on the highly colored and eventful old animal books, and I am made to realize how very *quiet* some

---

* In the matter of wild things' animal ingenuity, their displays of personality and their exercises sometimes of a wild wisdom which, compounding instincts, sensory awarenesses, learnings established by trial and error, and gifts animalwise for "getting the feel" of a situation, can issue in astonishing behaviors, I should particularly not want to seem merely contemptuously skeptical. If I am smiling here, it is only at the crashing vividness of the instances the old romancers always cited, and the ease with which they could always find, in any copse, manifestations of animals' kind of creature wisdom at its most dramatic. Animal personality, the thing itself, is real enough. Any neighborhood naturalist with long experience and insight must agree with Julian Huxley's view that it is as bad as exaggerating animals' personalities by anthropomorphizing them to underestimate and minimize them by "mechanomorphizing." Back when we were talking at length about animals' personalities, by the way, I spoke of the church's stern refusal of souls to animals. It is pleasant to note that Cardinal Newman, who was surely orthodox, permitted himself in this a considerable latitude. If animals, in his view, had not a human kind of souls, still they might have "tokens" thereof. Perhaps after all, in the deeps of eternity, there may be scampering a dim little blur that is the shade of White-foot, a deer mouse. Possibly in the Elysian fields, as in these daisy-starred and sun-warm ones that Mary and I know and love, there may sound a token whistle of our woodchuck neighbor.

of these readers must find this book in which Mary and I are telling about our animal neighbors and the experiences in which we have come to know them. I speak in these pages of an adventure, and it turns out to be only seeing a white-footed mouse scampering across an aspen clearing. I say that we have found something exciting or extraordinary, and it is only a muskrat nibbling a minnow in the dusk, or a woodchuck family playing rigmaroles in our pasture by the light of the moon. These must seem "small" things to some rememberers of how Silverpatch won his great fight with Cloud Wings the Eagle. But if this is to be a truthful book, it has to be said that it is precisely in small things that real animal knowing largely consists; and the "excitements" of intimacy with animal neighbors have the excitingness not so much of huge events as of the discovery of secrets.

Getting to know animal neighbors is a continual adventure precisely because there are *not* wild-life dramas in every thicket. To know muskrats with as much neighborly intimacy of detail as we do has taken Mary and me many, many years. To formulate the story even of our common woodchucks—even of omnipresent White-foot—means putting together hundreds, thousands, of discontinuous small observations and encounters. As I said a while ago, there are far more animals living in any piece of countryside than anyone but a naturalist might suspect. But they are not in continual parade. The lives of most wild creatures are largely lived hiddenly, or at least with such shyness or wariness that getting to know animal neighbors intimately is not a matter of just stepping into the outdoors and seeing them, but rather of long hours of patient silence, stillness, and waiting, and of unexpected little glimpses caught casually on innumerable occasions, and of a slowly deepening acquaintance and intimacy by a whole long program of discovery.

This is true even in the case of the biggest, in a sense most conspicuous, and undoubtedly most animally dramatic of all Mary's and my companioning animals here: our white-tailed deer.

A big buck deer weighs perhaps three hundred pounds and may stand some forty inches high at his red-brown shoulder. One of our deer neighbors, bounding easily through the hemlock woods on the hill, moves at a stressless twenty-five miles an hour or better. Charging away through the underbrush in alarm, a deer goes faster than that. Sailing in a great leap over a windfall, a Whitetail can describe an aerial arc spanning fifteen or twenty feet. In addition to deer's bigness, and thus, as it were, the outsize of everything about their lives, there is also this: Whitetails are devoted to one small patch of earth, even as are neighborhood naturalists themselves. A deer is happy on a range of half a square mile. Whitetails have lived out their lives, from fawnhood to death, without ever setting a pointed hoof outside the acres of our neighborhood. Drowsing away the sunny noontimes in beds in the tall fox grass up by Owl Rock, grazing at dawn on the east ridge, trotting down the familiar day-by-day deer trail at dusk to drink at the brook pool beyond the orchard—a Whitetail's life follows an ordered pattern as small as that. Our Whitetail neighbors, in a sense, are always with us here almost as little White-foot neighbors are. They "belong" in these woods and fields, where Mary and I are, and they scarcely leave them, except when bucks may travel outside in the restlessness of their autumns.

For all this, we have had to "discover" our Whitetails; and, for all this, our adventures in deer-knowing have mostly been of what I suppose may seem a quiet kind. There have been a few episodes of high, evident drama. I have already told how a wounded buck once came fearlessly to us, as if for sanctuary, and stood so close I could put my hand on him. Another time I was able to watch a doe in what must have been nearly the last hour of her life. But most of our excitements in getting to know our deer neighbors have lain in little things: in discovering those secret bits of deer behavior, those fragments of close "inside" deer information, that let us know our deer, instead of merely as animals whose general life story is easy enough to discern, as intimate personalities that we can take to us in a wealth of little particulars.

For instance, deer love water. They are strong swimmers—plunging across a pond or river not merely to escape an enemy but apparently sometimes just because they want to browse on the other side, or just for the joy of it—and in hot weather they love to lie in the shallows of a pond or the muddy ooze along its edge. The brook that runs through our acres is nowhere wide enough to make a pool that can be called a pond; and the marshy tract near Muskrat Pool has ooze hardly deep enough to comfort a Whitetail on a hot evening when the deer flies are biting. Must deer forgo their water pleasures in a neighborhood like ours? We found out otherwise one humid June dusk.

We were sitting on a brookside boulder, not keeping especially still in the hope of seeing an animal neighbor, but just talking quietly together and occasionally listening to a low tremolo *hoo-loo-looing* over in the edge of the dark woods which might have been either an owl or a coon.

Mary looked up along the watercourse in the deepening darkness.

"What a funny little scraggle of roots has piled into that little pool up there, just by the flycatcher tree." (The fly-catcher tree is an old apple tree, full of rot hollows, and for years crested flycatchers have nested every year in these holes, never failing to hang out, flycatcher-fashion, a snakeskin.)

I looked where she was looking. There was certainly a small irregular dark mass in the little brook pool. I couldn't remember having noticed it there the evening before. I stood up to walk to the pool and investigate.

As I got up, so did the small scraggle of roots. It got up with a *whoosh* and a splather of flying legs suddenly un-curled, and all at once it was enormous; and with a burst of clattering and splashing a Whitetail dashed away up the brook, its white signal-flag tail glimmering in the darkness.

We walked to the little rocky-sided pool where the deer had been lying—lying so deep and tightly fitted in that only its head and part of its shoulders had been showing. I should have been hard put to curl into that little water basin myself.

What does a deer do where there are no ponds or lakes? Well, *that's* what it does. It finds little natural bathtubs, and somehow squeezes itself impossibly tiny, and huddles happily inside them and dozes away the dusk.

That is the kind of little discovery I mean, the sort of neighbor-knowing that has in it, for naturalists like Mary and me, an excitement of secret revealed, of close-up experienced, that is as great, in its funny kind of poignance, as what excitement the old nature-romancers thought to find only in the spectacular.

Take another example. Whitetails are easy animals to watch. Having come to know the pattern and timetable of their lives, Mary and I go up early in the morning to see them browsing on the east ridge, or we go over to the upland pasture by the birch copse in the twilight, and unless the wind betrays us we can often watch our Whitetails at their quiet feeding for half an hour or more. Browsing deer cover territory only very slowly, and they stay within range a long while. When first we began our watchings of them, years ago, we used to stay continuously "frozen." When deer have their heads down, grazing, they are unnoticing and unsuspicious; but every so often, as if suddenly starting out of its grass-sweet dream and remembering vigilance, a deer throws up its head and stares alertly all around. We used to wish there were some way we could tell when a member of a herd was going to do this. If there were, we could relax our immobility a little without risking being caught by one of these sudden inspections. It was only after we had watched our deer neighbors many times that we came to the realization that a deer's sudden head-raising is hardly ever done without a warning.

The warning lies in a very little thing, a quirk of Whitetail personality. Nine times out of ten, a split second before a Whitetail lifts its head, it gives a nervous waggling flip of its seven-inch brushy tail. Whitetails are continually giving little flirts and twitches of their tails, of course; but this abrupt major waggle is unmistakable. Since Mary and I discovered it and what it signals, not only have we been able to be more relaxed in our hedgerow hiding places—shifting position, and even whispering together, in intervals between our deer's tail-flash signals—but we have felt an exciting increase in our neighborly intimacy, in the rapport established, psyche to psyche, between ourselves and these fellow beings of ours that share the woods and fields of this small world in its cleft of the hills.

I think of another little episode contributing to our discovering the deer.

I was out alone on a crisp October morning, scuffing through the fallen leaves and listening to the whitethroats. Over in the scrubland beyond the swamp by Muskrat Pool, I jumped a buck. As so often happens—in the real world of the deer we have known, if not in the tremendous tales of the naturalists of my boyhood—he did not crash away in a thundering flight off over the horizon. After his initial startled plunge from a little stand of maple saplings, he bounded in easy arcs only as far as the next patch of cover. This was a low growth of brushy alders, not more than a hundred feet away. The buck eased to a walk, slipped into this, and vanished.

I watched to see him emerge. He did not. I studied the alder tops for a glimpse of horns. There was none. I stood considerably puzzled, for the alders of the little thicket were hardly a yard high and I could not guess how a big buck could lose himself so entirely—could vanish under my eyes—in such a tiny and inadequate patch of shelter.

Many of our animal neighbors practice a "vanishing" trick that is one of the most familiar woods stratagems Mary and I encounter. Dodging behind a bush or a big tree trunk, an animal then runs away in an almost incredibly straight line, so that the bush or tree trunk is always kept between it and the eyes of the watcher. We have seen all sorts of our neighbors from squirrels to foxes "disappear" by this woods magic; and Whitetails are so expert in it that even a big buck can seem to be hiding, if you don't know better, behind a remarkably small tree or boulder, when in fact he has made beeline, under the cover of this visual obstacle, to new and better cover hundreds of yards off. There was no possible way, though, in which my buck could have used this deer-guile to get away from the low little thicket of alders. I couldn't see how he could have left, and I couldn't see how he could still be there, hidden completely, either.

I had a low-powered opera glass with me that morning, for I had gone out for casual bird-watching, not looking for animal neighbors. Standing perfectly still, I raised the glass very slowly to my eyes and studied the alder thicket inch by inch. I thought I saw something. Putting one foot before the other almost as slowly as a great blue heron wading along our brook in search of frogs and minnows, I moved toward the thicket, peering. Almost at the edge of it I stopped, stood tiptoe, and peered in. Yes. The buck was there. He had "vanished," when he slipped into this little low patch of brush, by instantly dropping to a knee crouch. He was still in this crouching position, huddled and hunched, and he was so confident of his invisibility that he did not move a muscle as I looked at him. I could see an eye, the soft tawny funnel of an ear, the spiked antlering of a buck probably three years old. With this much to "locate" him, I could trace out, in the checkering of the thicket, the rest of his outlined shape. If I had not known he was there, and so stared into the thicket in that almost certain knowledge and with the intensity of expectation, I could have sworn that a piece of cover so tiny and inadequate could not possibly conceal a deer. As slowly as I had approached, and with a new fragment of Whitetail understanding to treasure, I withdrew from my buck's hiding place, leaving him triumphant in the kneeling trick I had now learned about.

It has been in such small adventures and discoveries as these that Mary's and my neighbor-knowing of our White-tails has mostly consisted. In undramatic little encounter, in unexpected little intimate glimpse, we have been made to feel "taken into" the pattern and texture of the deer life lived around us.

The beginning of that life—the birth of Whitetail fawns —usually takes place in our neighborhood in May. May of course is the most consumingly wonderful month for any naturalist outdoors. It is too teeming to take in, and far too unutterably meaningful for us ever to be able to catch in words. This is the month when arbutus and bloodroot are blossoming in the dark leaf mold in our woods. It is the time for burying our noses in them, and snuffing the smell of our earth, and being flooded with assurance. This is the month when the phoebes are building, and the time for us to go poking under old bridges, to watch the birds at their building and to have our spirits strengthened and freshened by the smell of common brook water. In May our barn swallows are coming back; it is the season for us to slog around the wet barnyard, exultant in the good smells of cattle and dung and straw, and to go clambering up into the dim and glorious place that is a hayloft. May is the time for seeing warblers, as they come thronging the greening maples and elms: black and white warblers, black-throated green ones, chestnut-sided ones, redstarts. It is our opportunity to re-experience the start of enchanted surprise that is a part of the sunny sanity of childhood. The wrens are singing. They are singing, directly into our aboriginal ears, an information that all pessimists and pedants are mistaken, and that the life adventure is a greater and gladder thing than mere learnedness might ever surmise. The catbirds and orioles and indigo buntings are here in May, garter snakes are astir on sun-warmed ledges and our old stone walls, the lilacs are in bloom—it is all too big for seeing or saying. But perhaps the enchantment of May is most completely caught and focused, for Mary and me, in the birth of the Whitetail fawns.

A doe Whitetail may occasionally have her baby out in an open field, but ordinarily it is born in a hedgerow or a thicket at the edge of the woods. The first time a doe gives birth, she usually has just one fawn. In subsequent Mays she is likely to have twins. Whitetail at birth weighs scarcely more than five pounds. The fawn is all a sprawl of spindly little legs and a dapple of spotted coat to make it invisible in the sun-dapple of its birthplace.

The babies of some of our animal neighbors quickly become able to take care of themselves. Their whole life cycle is brief (I was saying, for instance, that one of our little white-footed mice grows up to become a parent itself within sixty days or so) but a deer doesn't reach its prime until it is five or six years old. Barring accidents, a hardy buck may bed in our hemlock woods and browse at dawn on the sunny eastern ridge for fifteen rounds of seasons. So young Whitetail matures slowly, in its grassy little form in the thicket, and for several weeks the fawn is primarily dependent for survival upon the concealing coloring of its spotted coat and upon obedience to its mother's instructions to stay quiet. Its dark little eyes have been wide open from birth, and it can stand, in a wobbly, unsteady way, on its long slim legs; but for at least the first two weeks of its life it rarely ventures more than a pace or two from the sheltering birth nest. Lying quiet, with its legs tucked under and its muzzle pressed down, the baby gives off scarcely any scent.

From soon after her fawn is born, a mother Whitetail leaves it alone a great deal of the time. Perhaps five or six times during a day, she returns to the thicket and nurses the youngster. After the first week or two, when it hears her coming, the fawn is likely to struggle to its feet and make a little stiff-legged prancing rush to meet her. She nuzzles it firmly and pushes it down; and if the fawn should be still hungry, or lonesome, when she starts to leave again, and should try to come straggling after her, she bunts it heavily until it drops down asprawl again in the concealing immobility that is its only real protection while the mother Whitetail is away.

In our years of making deer-discoveries, Mary and I have found little fawns just twice. It may seem a meager record. Some of the old naturalists of our childhood, I realize, would have found fawns in every Maytime thicket. But it is testimony to the effectiveness of baby deer's concealment, and to the effectiveness of Whitetail mothers' staying away from their little ones so much of the time and thereby not disclosing the home whereabouts. Once, high on our hill near Owl Rock, in a tangle of sumac and partridgeberry, we found a "form" with a fawn in it that could not have been much more than a week or ten days old. On the other occasion, which was at the edge of the woods we call the Squirrel Woods, in a warm June dusk, we met a somewhat older little fawn, wobbling and teetering all alone on what we suppose must have been only a short excursion from its home thicket. Both times Mary and I were made to feel that we had stepped "inside" our Whitetail neighbors' life with an intimacy as deep as can be reached.

We found our Owl Rock fawn entirely by accident, while I was scrabbling around on my hands and knees in the sun-hot underbrush trying to find a nest of towhees. Abruptly, three yards away, a pair of dark little deer eyes was looking into mine. I crouched perfectly still, on knees and hands, and felt overcome with reward for whatever may have been the occasional trials of a lifetime of being a naturalist. The fawn lay curled around, with its legs invisible to me, seeming scarcely bigger than a dapple-furred rabbit. It lay so motion-less, while we looked at each other, that it did not even blink. I could see its small body shaken by quick, shallow breaths, but otherwise it was just as immobile as a small fawn in a picture.

I held motionless until my knees and arms ached, staring into that wild little neighbor's alert dark eyes, and until at last Mary called out to know what I was doing. I whistled to her. Years ago she and I agreed upon a special whistle which we use on such occasions as this in our animal adventurings. After all, it isn't usual that we both see exactly the same thing at the same time outdoors. One of us makes the discovery, and must signal the other. A call or a spoken word, we learned long ago, is almost always frightening to any of our animal neighbors. It snaps the spell which "freezing" may have established. A high or shrill whistle is almost as bad. But a very low-pitched whistle, soft and long-drawn, seems to many of our animals scarcely to be associated with humanness. They only cock their heads a little, or prick their ears, as at anything strange, but don't apparently understand that the low soft sound is coming from the frozen watcher close at hand. So when either Mary or I discovers an animal neighbor of ours in sudden close-up, the discoverer gives this special long low whistle. "Come stealthily," it means. It sounds something like a mourning dove. (Or it's meant to; I am not a very good whistler, and Mary is a worse one.) I whistled now, from my crouch in the thicket, never taking my eyes off the small fawn. It gave no heed, only turning its narrow head a little at the first twig-crackle of Mary's approach. (Deer are not able to roll their eyes in their sockets. A Whitetail must keep turning its head to watch an object moving across its horizon.) Mary slipped catfooted into the thicket and dropped down, and we joined in such an enchanted half-hour of deer intimacy as we have never had again. We kept listening for a sound of the Whitetail mother's return, but she did not come.

Early the next day we were back on the hill, watching, this time from the shelter of some boulders on a knoll in the next field, using our binoculars. We watched for three days, seeing mother Whitetail come to the thicket to nurse her youngster, seeing her stand over it just as she was about to leave each time and "instruct" it to quietness by pressing it down into its bed with her nose and holding it like that, very still, for several seconds. It would have been easy to suppose that she was actually speaking to it, murmuring a deer message into those velvety funnel-shaped fawn ears.

The third day we spoiled everything. I suppose the sense of easy intimacy with our Whitetail's nursery had begun to make us a little careless, so that we relaxed the motionlessness of our watch from behind the rocks. We had just watched mother Whitetail come to give a feeding. As always, she approached her fawn's hiding place at a slow, circuitous, cautious walk, stepping deftly among the sidehill birch saplings with scarcely a sound, throwing up her head and looking searchingly around at nearly every step, and at last gliding into the thicket as quietly as a shadow. Mary or I must have craned a neck too abruptly to see the meeting of mother and baby—a lovely thing to see, the fawn all tottery and tremulous with welcome, the doe nuzzling and cat-licking it and somehow, motherwise, surrounding it in protection and reassurance—or one of us may have kicked a loose pebble or

I-don't-know-what. Abruptly the head of a doe was raised up and was staring tensely straight at us.

Crash! There was a plunging and thudding, and in what seemed like a split second, from perhaps fifty yards' distance from the nursery thicket, there exploded the doe's urgent warning bark.

Deer are often thought of as virtually voiceless animals, and in casual encounters no doubt they usually are; but Mary and I, knowing our Whitetails neighbor-close over the years, have not found them so. A doe trying to round up a strayed fawn often bleats loudly enough to be heard a considerable distance through our summer woods. Any deer, when it comes suddenly on a startling or suspicious thing and wants, as it were, to test the situation, may huff and chuff in a noisy kind of snorting. Once in the deep snow of February, I remember, I jumped a buck in the very deepest part of our hemlock woods, and as he labored away among the snow-bowed evergreens he made a high, thin, moaning exclamation almost like a scream. The deer sound Mary and I hear oftenest is the "bark" that exploded now from the Whitetail mother. It is a violent, breathy blast, with a queerly resonant kind of timbre in it. What it most sounds like, I think, is the noise you can make by holding a grass-blade stretched between the thumbs of your cupped hands and blowing on it.

As our startled doe sounded her alarm cry again and again —*kaa! kaa! ka-haaaa!*—Mary and I came out from behind our boulders, letting her see us plainly, and hurried off down the hill for home. The little glimpse she had had of us, in our hiding place, had perhaps had the specially terrifying quality of the Unknown; and now if she could see us as just the familiar naturalists of the place, reasonably expectable at any hour in the top of a tree or popping up from behind a swamp tussock, it might be a reassurance to her.

The harm had been done, though. When we climbed the hill to the thicket the next day, our fawn was gone from its nursery. The mother must have led and nudged and nuzzled it to a new and safer hideaway. It probably wasn't far away, even now, and we might have found it again by a careful hunt through the greenery over an acre or so; but though intimacy with our animal neighbors is what we love better than anything else in the world, we don't like intimacy to become intrusion; so we made no search. After all, as we said to each other as we swung down the hill, listening to the tow-hees scrabbling in the hedgerows and hearing the chickadees make the funny little tattered song that is all that remains of their voice in that season, we had already had such an adventure in deer-closeness and deer-discovery as should content us.

Our other meeting with a small fawn, in a dusk at the edge of the Squirrel Woods, was a much briefer adventure; but there was a great poignance packed in it, and we have talked of it many times.

("But what do you do on the long winter evenings, in that lonely country place of yours?" people sometimes ask. Well,

among other things, we remember. Neighborhood naturalists store up recollections for wintertime, as gray squirrels store
up hickory nuts. Our house is full of small remembrances: a
vireo nest with some of White-foot's cherry pits in it, a spray
of deer-browsed alder, a smooth stone on which at Muskrat
Pool we watched a drenched neighbor sit grooming his water-
sleek fur. Around all these things cluster recollections of adventurings, and there are hosts of other recollections that have
no tangible souvenirs. "What do you do on the winter evenings?" It is no problem, when the fireplace glows and flickers with a blaze of smoky-sweet apple logs, and when you
have had years of storing and treasuring the memories of
happy explorations of a neighborhood outdoors, to find a large
contentment in the serenity of doing nothing at all.)

This little fawn was standing stock-still beside the mossy
bole of a big hemlock tree, and we came upon it so abruptly
in the twilight that we nearly bumped into it. I should think
it was not old enough to have wandered very far by itself
through the evening woods world. It was probably just on a
somewhat overextended exploratory roam from its hidden
birthplace. As we swung around the hemlock tree and came
upon it—literally, as I say, almost stumbling over it—the
fawn stood absolutely motionless.

What any animal will do in given circumstances is always
in a sense unpredictable. There is the course that the animal
is "supposed" to take, textbookwise; and then there is the
course that you have perhaps familiarly seen it take before in

similar circumstances; and then finally there is the course that it may take now, unpredictable and perhaps unprecedented. The fact that animals are personalities—at least in the way I have tried so often in these pages to define and delimit—and accordingly are not entirely confined in the "must" of automatism, is what gives an everlasting element of surprise and novelty to all animal-adventurings. Meet a small fawn, face-to-face in the dusk, and what will he do? It can be written in no book of rules. It can only be adventured, in this time and place, now.

What our fawn did this time was immediate, and nearly sent Mary into tears. It took a halting step toward her, lifted its head, and stood trustful and hopeful. Gently, slowly, she stretched out her forefinger, in the gesture wherewith she brings peace and assuagement to very small heifers when they are first introduced, bewildered and bereft of mother, to our pasture. The fawn reached up, nibbled the finger into its mouth, and with a tiny whoofling bleat of fulfillment settled to an absorbed nursing.

It could scarcely have lasted ten seconds. When we first came upon the fawn, it had taken us to be something as natural to the woods and unalarming as our visiting Whitefoot one winter had apparently found us. It had still felt so, apparently, when it sniffed and took Mary's finger. But almost in the instant that it received the proffered pacifier into its mouth, it must have been flooded with a knowing—a tremendous inrushing knowing, as through its whole organ-

ism and right down to the center of its little fawn psyche—
that something was enormously and terribly amiss.

Our fawn collapsed.

I have never seen a comparable collapse except once when
a tree-dwelling sloth, accustomed to hanging upside down
from the undersides of branches, was stood right-side-up on
the ground. The sloth simply flumped asprawl, with what
seemed to be ten or fifteen legs sliding helplessly in all directions. Our fawn did exactly this now. At one instant it was
standing, happy and fulfilled, nibbling and sucking away at
a finger, while Mary and I looked at each other and held our
breaths. The next instant, seized and overwhelmed by the
inrush of fearful knowledge, the fawn lay sprawled in the
leaf mold and moss, its slim legs flung out in disarray, its little
head pressed flat down, its whole look—except that its dark
eyes were open, and gleaming—the look of death.

We hesitated only a second, collecting ourselves from the
shock of this vivid possum-playing, and then we hurried
away, tiptoe, out of the edge of the woods and off across the
open fields through the deepening darkness. We have often
wondered how long the fawn stayed collapsed in the shadowy
woods by the hemlock tree—how long it took for the reced-
ing, from its dim and confused little fawn mind, of the spirit-
shaking discovery that not everything in this green garden of
the world is always exactly what it seems.

The fawns of our neighborhood stay with their mothers all
summer, learning what woods lore they need (which cannot

often include the discovery of human fingers), and in winter become mixed into the general company of adult bucks, does, and fellow first-year fawns from other birthplaces in our neighborhood's thickets and hedgerows.

The bucks during the summer are alone, or occasionally in a small group. This is their season for antler-growing. Our buck Whitetail neighbors start their growth of antlers quite early in spring, about the time, as it happens, when fawns are being born. From little swellings on a buck's forehead, just in front of its ears, the antlers slowly grow to be rounded velvety stubs, then into antler-shape (but still staying soft, warm, blood-filled and blunt), and finally by the latter part of summer they become bone-hard and are scraped free of the last bits and shreds of the soft skin in which they have come to maturity. Just before autumn begins, Mary and I often go looking through our woods for a "deer tree," sometimes a sapling, sometimes a big rough-barked trunk, against which a buck Whitetail has rubbed and frayed the lingering velvet from his hardening horns. The shedding skin must be an itching annoyance, for a buck tries to scrape it off as soon as it starts shriveling and while it is still blood-fed. Sometimes I have found a place where it has seemed certain, at first, that some bloody battle must have taken place; and then in a minute I can see the bits of deer velvet, and the heart-shaped hoofprints in the woods loam, and I know that it is only where a buck has stopped to clash and polish his antlers and free them of the fretting particles of their skin of immaturity.

Our Animal Neighbors

In November and December our Whitetails come to their season of rut, and there is initiated the new generation of little fawns to be born some seven months later. By midwinter or a little after, bucks' antlers loosen and drop off. By now the whole deer company is in quiet association—bucks, does, and the fawns of the spring before—and so it stays until time for the next generation.

Such are Mary's and my Whitetail neighbors, companioning us over the years and around the seasons. Big neighbors as they are, they are such quiet sharers of this countryside, so adept in concealment and such lovers of the half-light of dawn and dusk, that we have had to get to know them by a long program of discovery. It is a discovery, as I have said, that has mostly lain in "little" things, an intimacy reached in quiet episodes that may disappoint rememberers of the old dramatic tales about titanic fights of antler-locked bucks in the Christmas snow and fabulous guiles exercised by does in protecting their spotted fawns in the green Maytime coverts. But we have loved every moment of our companionship with deer, however quiet.

One spring evening, at a woods opening on our western slope where there used to be a wagon trail, a doe and twin fawns stood behind a great maple tree and all peered out around its vast trunk at Mary and me as we walked by. The three heads of our watchers were all that was visible. They were grouped close together, as in a clover-leaf cluster, and they were silhouetted against the fading yellow-crimson of the sunset sky. That's all there was to the episode; but I should consent to part with the remembrance of it only very dearly. On any evening, as likely as not, we can watch White-tails come to our brook to drink, and often can steal close enough to hear their plash and ripple as they dip their dark muzzles in the cool flowing water. It is a little thing to have as accompaniment to your days; but we find an unending loveliness and pleasure in it. We watch our deer flag-signaling with their tails, as a group troops to the edge of the dirt road and prepares to cross; or we see a buck just standing on a snow-swept November ridge, tossing his antlers and pawing and snuffing the frosty autumn air; or we slog through the drifts up the wood road on a bitter January day and find the "beds" of our Whitetails, dry and inviting in the evergreen shelter, with scatterings of deer droppings all around and a sense as of a deer "village," there among the snow-laden con-ifers; and none of this is a little thing to neighborhood natu-ralists like Mary and me. It is an excitement to be neighbor-intimate even with a white-footed mouse (who, by the way, is a great eater of bucks' shed antlers; we have found antlers in our woods that were all fretted into lacework by White-foot's gnawings); but fellowship with our biggest animals seems to carry in a particular fashion a special excitement of its own.

Even the largest and most dramatic of my experiences with Whitetail, may not, I realize, have been a very large ad-venture in one sense. But to me, in a profound sense, it was very large, for what thoughts it started. It happened very early on a summer morning, just past dawn.

I had gone up nearly to the top of our hill, to a steep overgrown field that slopes down to a hemlock hollow where there is a never-drying pool. I had gone alone. Among the reasons Mary adduces for her not being properly describable as a naturalist—such reasons as her indifference to species names, and her disinterest in those aspects of animal knowledge that suggest the formally scientific or an "ology"—there is the fact that she dislikes getting up before sunrise. She will do it, and has done it a good many times over the years; but she cannot pretend to an enthusiasm for it. The nuns in Irish schools, says Mary, have a way of thinking that a new day should begin practically in the middle of the night, and they impose this conviction in a set of rules upon their small charges. In her grown-up years, Mary says, she needs to try to catch up on some of the thousands of hours of childhood rest she missed. She will get up in darkness for our warbler migrations and for a few other inestimably precious sunrise happenings outdoors; and she will cheerfully *stay* up, mosquito-eaten, night-chilled and motionless, on our animal vigils in the darkness, until hints of the next day begin to lighten the sky; but in exploration of the world of sunrise I mostly go alone.

The flooding lightness that comes just before sunup was upon the sloping field, as I sat cross-legged on the ground among concealing maple saplings at the edge of it. I had been sitting there only a little while, watching the diffusion of white light turn to gold light from the east, when two does came into my range of vision. They were nibbling and browsing in only a desultory way, and were mostly engaged in a kind of running tease of playfulness, bunting each other, making little rushes and prances, then pausing for a brief resumption of nibbling the still night-cool vegetation. They were full of the glory of the morning.

I looked hard and could hardly believe what I saw.

From the belly of one of the does a great stub or spike of dead branch was projecting.

Sometime that night or morning she had made a sailing deerlike leap, had missed her footing or miscalculated, and had impaled herself on this great sword of jagged deadwood. It had broken off, and now she was trailing this monstrous thing in her. I looked hard, catching my breath, and I could see that she was bleeding heavily. (Later I followed part of her blood-trail; it seemed impossible that she could have lost so much.) Before sunset of this day, probably much sooner, she would undoubtedly be dead.

Now, in the sunrise, she was feeding and playing. There was no terror at all in the mind in that graceful skull from which the little light of deer-consciousness would so soon wink out. There was no wince of pain, nor any foreboding. There was no dark shadow cast before to darken this sunrise. I stared and stared at my mortally wounded doe, watching her with a hardly breathing intensity while she browsed and played with her companion and now and then looked out over the panorama of the lowlands with her calm eyes. I wanted to take to me every minute of her, until she disappeared over the brow of the field, still reposed in her unbreakable animal confidence, still stepping to the music of animal play. For I was made in these moments to know something that I have known as a naturalist for many years, but never so well as now, so bone-deep.

> Then sing, ye Birds, sing, sing a joyous song!
> And let the young Lambs bound
> As to the tabor's sound!
> We in thought will join your throng,
> Ye that pipe and ye that play. . . .

Thus Wordsworth.

Until a century or so ago, writers about nature wrote very largely in this mood of rejoicing and alleluia. Nature was seen as all goodness and gladness, birds and beasts as happy innocents frolicking forever in a perpetuated Garden of Eden. Birds sang in exuberance and praise; animals romped and frisked and went the good ways ordained for them; the natural world (if excepting, it might be, ourselves) was everywhere a scene of everlasting playing and paean.

Since the scientific theories of Charles Darwin burst into the public consciousness, this view of nature has been steadily dwindling and yielding place to another. In the celebrated verbal duel, now almost a hundred years ago, between Professor T. H. Huxley and Bishop Wilberforce of Oxford, the defender of Christian orthodoxy unmistakably made in some respects a fool of himself. Public faith in the book of Genesis, and presently in the whole scheme of religious traditionalism, being thereby badly shaken, it was natural enough that a kind of catchword Darwinism should become the new popular philosophy. Bishop Wilberforce had insisted that God looked upon the creation and found it good. Bishop Wilberforce had been proved, in controversy, to be sometimes unscientific. What more natural, therefore, than to reject the whole vision of a primal paradise, a world originally good and happy, and espouse instead a new scientific view, easily sloganized in the Darwinian phrases "struggle for survival" and "survival of the fittest?"

So it has happened. The romantics and the Victorians have died away. Few poets write, any more, Wordsworthian idylls about happy lambs that bound as to a tabor. Birds are understood to sing not for joyousness, in an innocency of spontaneous lauds, but only for the practical purpose of staking off a claim to a nesting territory as a part of the struggle for survival. Modern man does not see nature any more in terms of a Garden of Eden, or hear the sounds of nature as the far sweet fluting of a Panpipe, or feel himself under any such spell as that of the dream of Isaiah. Nature is one great struggle, very likely purposeless. It is all turmoil and blood and death. The lamb is not leaping as to a tabor. He is probably leaping because he is afflicted with sheep bots.

Now there can be no doubt that the long traditional view of the world of nature and the spirit of animal life did sometimes sentimentalize and falsify. It sometimes saw the natural world too pretty and pastel; it played down the pungent realities of blood and sweat and excrement and birth and death. But for all this tendency, in its bad moments, to a certain mood of pious vapidity and simper, the old paradisal vision must recommend itself to a naturalist as a great deal truer, a great deal deeper in insight, than the struggle-and-misery vision which has succeeded it. So Mary and I know; so every naturalist knows, who is much outdoors among his fellow animals, with his mind clear and candid; so I was made to know most piercingly and bone-deep, in the sunrise, watching my doe. Bishop Wilberforce, very likely, subscribed to many errors. But he was not in error in thinking that animal life is happy life. William Wordsworth may have promulgated much pathetic fallacy. But he was not fallacious when he held that the spirit of his birds and beasts was the spirit of joy and play. For without sentimentality and without argument, it is the fact.

A man may take what view he likes of the Book of Genesis and of the similar accounts of the creation that foundation other great religious traditions. He may think this or that one divinely underwritten; or he may think them all legends and poetry. But the vision on which they all commonly insist—the vision of a primal goodness and gladness in which all the beasts are caught up as in a song of joy—that vision is no creation of woolly-witted mysticism. It is a lyric statement of the simple truth as a naturalist knows it.

The spirit of animal life is the spirit of happiness. Looked at from above, with our human eyes, animals' foragings and preyings, fightings and dyings may seem to be a struggle and may even seem (so sick are we sometimes in our own wretchedness) to be a tragedy. But as experienced by the animal, life presents itself in no such terms.

Animals leap into combat joyously, confident in their strength and obedient to the surge of their impulse of assertion; for it can cross no animal's mind that it may lose. Animals lie down, mortally wounded, without any of the fear that has been known to make even archbishops whimper on their deathbeds; for it cannot enter an animal's mind that it is going to die. Animals contract diseases and undergo injuries, but no animal experiences what we mean by suffering; for the experience of pain is in ratio to the quality of attentiveness and high consciousness in the mind. A sick man, lying quiveringly alert in bed, may faint from the pain of some trivial manipulation by his doctor. The same man, fleeing a burning building and intent only on that engrossing necessity, may break his arm and gash his skull open and never notice any pain at all. An animal cannot recall the past in anguish and regret; an animal cannot peer imaginatively into the future and dread what it may hold. An animal lives in Now.

Living continually in Now, feeling the biddings of the

senses and acting with sublime confidence upon them as they come—this is the quality of animal life. It is strange we can ever lose sight of it; for we have all been children; and a small child, in the limitation of his understanding and the robust joy he takes in the sensory excellences of Now, is very much an animal. Life for an animal is now the good smell of the earth, and now the good hotness of the sun, and now the fine passionate urge to breed, and now the sweet fury and blood-taste of a fight, and now the closing in of a not-understood and not-feared darkness that means that death has come. In a life like this, there is no place for fear as we know fear. There is no place for sorrow as we know sorrow. There cannot be shame. There cannot be guilt. There can be only the eager quiver of aliveness and response. The world is all immediacy and acquiescence.

Spared, by the nature of their consciousness, all the weary welter of fear and pain and indecision and remorse, animals turn as naturally to playing as little children do, in their confident strength and faith and gladness to be alive.

Otters make mud slides on the grassy banks leading down to the water; and player after player, flat on his furry belly, with his forelegs folded back, goes whizzing delightedly down the slide and *whomps* into the water. Bears wrestle and tumble and cuff each other and roll upon the ground in ecstasies of high spirits. Our rabbit neighbors here, in the moonlight, leap dementedly over one another's backs, daft with the delirious business of being able to smell the scent of the dew-wet grass and of being able to feel the strength of lithe muscles and being alive in the splendor of Now. Lambs, as in the accurate hosanna-song of William Wordsworth, skip and run and leap for no other reason than the exuberant outburst of lambness; nor can the presence of sheep bots, which no lamb's mind is equipped to understand or pay attention to, damp these high ardors.

The world of animals is everywhere a world of play, even as it is a world, by the nature of its consciousness, of sureness and security. The most improbable animals play. A badger has a look of stodginess and gravity; but a naturalist crony of Mary's and mine out in Wisconsin has described an uproarious game played by a badger and a dog. A fox, five minutes after he has eluded the hounds (and even *that* grim adventure is treated by many foxes in a spirit of hilarity), may amuse himself, all alone in the green woods, by tossing twigs up in the air and catching them in his mouth. I have known of raccoons that playfully pelted pebbles at a flock of chickens. Coyotes play something very like a children's game of hide-and-seek; mountain goats go coasting down snow slides, with fine lusty roughs-and-tumbles together when they all get to the bottom; and W. H. Hudson recorded many observations in support of his surprising discovery that there is a tremendous playfulness among the pumas of La Plata. Perhaps, at that, the discovery should have come as no great surprise. For all cats play, the great wild ones as well as the small domestic ones. Exuberation and delight in living run through all the world of the animals, from the lioness twitching her tail tip to furnish an exciting plaything for her cubs to the little meadow mouse rushing up a weed stalk and down again in an antical game of tag with a meadow-mouse companion. Play is in all the woods and all the meadows and all the prairies everywhere. It is in this neighborhood of Mary's and mine, a persisting music.

No naturalist, of course, can think of denying Charles Darwin's findings about the competitions and adaptations that occur in the world of nature, or can regard with anything but solemn respect Darwin's patient investigation of the modes and methods by which these processes go forward. But what requires to be understood and remembered is that the use in this connection of the word struggle—with all its implications of distress, fear, worry, and grim effort—is at least as anthropomorphic as any theological conception of the much-derided Bishop Wilberforce. It is a projection into animal life of the quality of our own consciousness.

It is an affair of much effort and sweaty terror for a middle-aged philosopher to walk along the top rail of a spike-topped picket fence. But we are obviously in serious error if we imagine that it is a thing of difficulty and alarm for a small boy to do so. For the boy it is all confident high spirits and good fun. Learned university graduates, holding innumerable degrees to prove that they are philosophers, may find it an exhausting and terrifying business to sleep on the ground in the wilderness and listen in the black night to the hoot of owls

and the squall of foxes. A boy on a camping trip finds it delightful. If a boy's consciousness has not yet taken on the load
of faithless misgiving and imaginative anxiety that can come
with adult mind, a fox's consciousness is further still below
that threshold, and a bird's still further, and a turtle's still
further than that.

Animal life requires consideration on two levels. There is
the matter of what animals *do;* and in this field a Darwin is
not to be contradicted. There is also the matter of what animals *experience;* and in this area the empathic boyhood-
remembering and understanding of a poet like Wordsworth,
or of the author of Genesis or of the singers of the earliest
Indian creation songs, may achieve a profoundly accurate insight that is a part of total truth as essential as any of the
chartings of science.

Up in the icy Arctic waters polar bears splash and cavort
in high glee. Down under the tropical sun big cats romp and
race as ecstatically as household kittens. Everywhere between
there is to be found the telling testimony of animal play.
There is to be found the telling testimony of a Whitetail doe,
with a spike in her belly and her blood spilling out, exulting
in the sunrise. This testimony seems immensely important
to Mary and me, and one of the invaluable reminders vouchsafed to neighborhood naturalists like us. For it tells a truth
at once vital to scientific accuracy in animal understanding
and to a kind of spiritual accuracy in any large reading of the
world. What it tells is that the goodness or the wretchedness

147

of life is a matter of the state of the mind. What it tells is the very old and enduring truth that the fruit of the tree of knowledge is a perilous fruit which none but our humankind has eaten.

Even this "biggest" of my Whitetail adventures, I realize, now that I have told it, was a big one for me rather in significance than in the thing itself. It has perhaps been so with nearly all Mary's and my animal knowings together. But at any rate, if our deer have not performed for us as startlingly as the ones in our childhood books, they have behaved in ways that have given us, in our own fashion, immense delight—and high excitement too—in their company. Lying awake in bed at night, we hear the familiar *clop-clop-plash* of our Whitetails, come to the brook to drink. Strolling in the evening, we have a trio of Whitetails peer out at us, soft-eared and gentle-eyed, from behind a maple tree. We have the knowledge, all around our years, that the Whitetails are close to us, companioning, even when we cannot see them. It is a knowledge in which we live with peculiar happiness.

A House of Coons

If you live long enough in the same small patch of woods and fields and explore this world continually, you come to such a familiarity with it that you know by heart almost every tree in the woods, every moss-green stone along the brook, nearly every sprig of wild geranium or cinquefoil in the meadow borders. Daily excursions into such a world are excursions into a landscape almost as much a part of you as the landscape of your mind. But there is never a monotony for naturalists such as Mary and I.

Our Animal Neighbors

For one thing, of course, a naturalist is sufficiently in love with the outdoors that he can never have enough of it. He can take and retake the same elm tree to him, the same phoebe calling and twitching its tail on the same sunny barn ridge, the same deer he saw yesterday and the same muskrat he expects to see tomorrow, and never possess or absorb these things sufficiently to be fulfilled. Beyond this, however, there is the fact that it is only by the long intimacy of daily familiarity that you can get to know a piece of countryside well enough to be immediately aware of any change in it, any new thing. Mary and I might put it something like this, I think: There is always something new under the sun, but the conditioning for making this discovery lies in knowing how things were under the sun of yesterday.

The old wood road that starts at the woods' edge just behind our house and climbs nearly to the top of the hill has for years been nearly a daily path for us. Day by day by day, we make our way up along this dim green trail in spring and summer, this snow-drifted, deer-hoof-printed white trail in winter, this smoky-golden trail that is all a pungence of hickory nuts and withering oak leaves in the autumns. By long, long familiarity, we know exactly where everything is and what to expect to see where. I can look with an instructed eye for new birds' nests, for I know where all the old ones are. If the bulky crow's nest in one of the high oaks has a new strand of fresh roots or a wisp of green leaves built into it, we are alerted to it at once; for that was not there yesterday. On a length of rotting old hickory trunk, a short way up the trail, gray squirrels sometimes come to sit for a spell of nut-shucking. Just glancing at the pattern of the scattered husks on this forest dining table, we know in an instant whether there has been activity since yesterday, for we studied the same spot sharply then and took it into our minds. The old wood road is profoundly familiar to us; and by virtue of that we can walk it daily and discover new things.

Hummingbirds' nests are sometimes said to be hard to find, for the tiny walnut-sized cup of mottled lichens and plant down looks like only a little bark bump on the branch to which it is fastened. But Mary and I have found a good many of them. We have done so because the bark bumps and branch shapes of all our trees up along the wood road are such a minutely familiar pattern to us, if only in the subconscious of our minds, that even a very tiny change leaps out at us and cries for notice. Again, I went up the wood road in the near darkness of a late June evening to investigate an uproar of alarms—*whit-whit! whit-whit!*—among the wood thrushes somewhere in the leafy twilight there. It was because even in the darkest gloaming the look of this woods place is so familiar to me that I could tell that the irregular little dark shape on top of a hemlock stub was not a part of the splintered wood. It was a baby screech owl. I was able to stand close enough to touch him. At my low whistle, Mary came quickly through the darkening woods and joined me. We stood a long while in the company of this almost tailless youngster, talking to him and delighting in the owlishness of him, while his mother glided back and forth on her soundless wings above us, snapping her beak and occasionally uttering a cautionary hoot. We learned something new about owls, by the way, that evening. At first we thought our owlet on the hemlock stub was keeping perfectly quiet. But then, when we put our heads very close to him—within a foot and a half or two feet, I should say—we discovered that in fact he was continually making a tiny sound of commentary, so soft as to be almost inaudible. It was the rolling *oolooloolool* of an adult screech owl, but diminished to a secret whisper.

It is because the old wood road is so intimately familiar to Mary and me that we discovered, the way we did, our house of coons. This was on an early summer afternoon, when we had gone strolling up the wood road just for the coolness of it, to hear the liquid notes of the thrushes in the greenery and the long-drawn pensive callings of the wood pewees from the deeply shadowed places. We discovered our coon neighbors' homestead (to be exact, Mary did) because of a piece of suet.

About three-quarters of the way up the old wood road, roughly opposite the place identified in our private geography as the Chickadee Stump, there stands a somewhat dwarfed but ancient oak midway between the trail and the little brook that flows through the bottom of the ravine. This oak is alive but it has a big hollow in its main trunk some twenty feet from the ground, probably dating back to a long-ago day when a side branch broke off and rain water began collecting in the break. Over the years, the hollow has extended perhaps two feet down inside the tree trunk, and the edges of its opening have healed over to make it look almost like a designed doorway.

It is a wonderfully promising-looking hollow to any naturalist with an eye for animal neighbors, and for years I have climbed up to it regularly and had a hopeful look inside. At one time or another the oak hollow has sheltered deer mice, a family of flickers, and downy woodpeckers on bitter winter nights. I had last looked into it, before this summer afternoon, the preceding autumn. The oak hollow was then tenantless. In our nearly daily walks up the wood road this spring and summer, now, we had of course always taken a sharp glance at the hollow as we passed by; but there had been nothing to see.

"Look!" cried Mary, and pointed upward.

On the bottom edge of the oak-tree door there was a little piece of something gray-white.

Staring at it, we could make out that it was a fragment of suet, undoubtedly salvaged either from the summer vestiges left in the bird feeder outside my study window or else from our refuse pit over in a distant part of the woods.

"How did *that* get up there?"

I expressed the confident guess that it had been wedged there by a crow or a jay or possibly by a gray squirrel. I was pondering aloud, in a wordy way, what deductions a naturalist might make to establish the best guess among these three, when the piece of suet began wobbling. A little gray "hand," with long nimble fingers, reached up from inside the oak hollow, curled around the piece of suet, and tugged at it. The lump of suet wobbled and bobbled again, then disappeared from view into the dark hollow. While we stood motionless, craning our necks upward and staring, there appeared in the hole opening, staring back at us, the Teddy-bear-eared, black-masked face of a raccoon.

I suppose if it were necessary to describe a coon to someone who had never seen one, the best way would be to say that it looks like a small bear, with a ring-striped tail and a burglar mask across its face. Actually, of course, no bear has a furry, banded tail, and no bear has a face anything like a coon's at all, and certainly no bear goes climbing with delicate skill far out on slim branches and delicate twig tips the way raccoons can. Still, even in strict zoological terms, there is a blood relationship between bearkind and coonkind; and the suggestion of this kinship somehow comes through vividly when you meet the living coon as your neighbor in your fields and woods.

Procyon lotor (*lotor:* the washer) has been one of the most delighting of Mary's and my animal neighbors, and the delight has partly lain, I am sure, in his small-bearishness. It was a keen disappointment to Mary to find that our countryside had no bears in it (no real bears, that is, no bear-sized bears). She had thought, from American animal tales of her

childhood and particularly from some yarns of James Fenimore Cooper, that almost any copse in this country could be
expected to produce a bear as readily as a moccasined Indian.
She has been reconciled to our lacks, at least in part, by our
having as neighbors the black-masked little bears that are
our raccoons.

Weighing fifteen or twenty pounds, a coon is a grizzly,
bushy-furred little prowler along our brook in the darkness,
among the cornfields on moonlit nights in latter summer
when the ears are ripening, and all over our countryside in the
black nights of snowy winter when food is hard to find. He
is one of the most strictly nocturnal of all our animal neighbors. Nearly all our animals, to be sure, prefer darkness or
the half-light of dusk or dawn for making their explorations
of the world, but I cannot recall that we have ever met even
one foraging raccoon in daylight. Nighttime is coon time.
When the moon comes up over our hemlock-dark hill, and
owls begin quavering and whippoorwills calling—then is
when Mary and I can go out along our glimmering brook
and expect to meet black-masked little bears. They love the
dampness as they love the dark. They come ambling along
the muddy banks, snuffling and sniffing and peering into the
shining water, and every now and then hunching very still
and gravely feeling around under the water with their long-
fingered forepaws in an exploratory fishing.

A walking coon steps bear-fashion, which is to say flat-
footed. Most of our animal neighbors bend their feet to throw

weight on their toes. "Digitigrade," the formal word is. But for a coon it is "plantigrade." Our little bear presses his whole foot flat against the earth at each step. While waddling and paddling along this way, he holds his plump body curiously high from the ground. The result is a kind of rolling coon gait unlike the walk of any of our other animals, though perhaps most like a skunk's. Coons, as Mary puts it, *trundle*. So they do; and the mark of their trundling passage is one of our favorite trails to see in the oozy mud of the brookside or in the fresh snow on a winter morning. A coon's paw-prints look astonishingly like the pattering footsteps of a barefooted tiny child.

If you devote your lifetime to knowing animals well, being intimate with them as neighbors or brothers and trying with all your scientific understanding and outgoing imagination to participate in their life experiences, it becomes less and less reasonable to think of any animal as malevolent. An animal does what its nature prompts it to do, in unresistance and acquiescence; and this program of creaturely enjoyment is a pleasant program of simple-hearted innocence, as much if the creature is a weasel with an appetite for hot blood, as if it is a white-footed mouse with an appetite for weed seeds. Mary and I find it impossible to feel that a snake, with its cold, elongated body looped along our stone wall, looks "sinister." What it looks like, and what it is, is a maliceless neighbor of ours enjoying, in a dim snake-relish, the blessing of the sun; and if it presently takes a kicking frog in its recurved teeth, that is no less a naturality than when our neighbor woodchuck takes an aster top for his supper. I was talking in the last chapter about how animals are spared, by the limitation of their understanding, imaginative anxiety and the kind of pain that can attach to foreknowledge. In the same way, an animal is shut away from the possibility of calculated evil. It can be itself, and in no way untrue to that. So what its life amounts to is the natural exercise of what are, for it, the natural goods; and this gives to all animal life a quality of repose in spontaneity, a kind of untroubled rejoicement in things as they are, that affords one of the happiest restorations to be derived by naturalists like Mary and me from intimacy with these neighbors.

Though all our animals are in this wide sense innocent, some of them, Mary has remarked, seem even more innocent than others. A gentle, delighted relish in being, a placid animal happiness in the excellence of how crayfish taste and how the woods night smells, a quality of child-happy inquiry and enthusiasm—all these are bundled together in one plump package in our ring-tailed little "bear" with the black mask.

A coon has teeth as formidable as a dog's. A hunted coon, shaken out of a tree, can land snarling and slashing and sometimes kill or disable two or three hounds in as many minutes. But except in such dire circumstances, a coon never uses its formidable equipment to any such ends. What our coon neighbor loves is just to trundle and putter along the brook, under the moon, sniffing the dampness and the night, dipping for underwater morsels, and being at peace. A coon's long nonretractile claws are massive enough to rake open the belly of even a big adversary in a fight. What a coon does with them is just scratch up seed mounds in our fields or go clambering around in the dark treetops, chirping and churring and relishing the dark. The fat little bear with the monkey hands and the burglar mask goes trundling through life in an enormous equability of being just his mild-spirited, quizzical-faced, coon self.

I met one of our coons over behind the barn one autumn night, as he was padding along over toward the brook. In customary coon fashion, he remained lost in his twilit coon thoughts of flowing water, crayfish, and green-skinned frogs, and acknowledged me only by turning his course through the pasture grass slightly aside so we would pass each other at a decent distance. On an impulse, just to see what would happen, I abruptly sat down cross-legged on the ground and emitted a comradely squeak to my fellow wayfarer through the night.

The coon halted at once and looked around at me. His finely drawn little head with the Teddy-bear ears was raised up high, and he thrust an inquiring, sharp little muzzle in my direction. I chirped and clucked at him again and sat still.

The coon came pattering toward me without hesitation, uttering as he came a soft little inquiring mumble: *oonk-oonk-oonk-oonk?*

He came straight up to me, placed two long-fingered little hands on my knee, and looked expectant.

As must have been made plain in this book by now, both Mary and I have a passion for touching—physically touching, laying a hand upon—the animal neighbors we are devoted to knowing. Things are possessed by a touch as by a name, but with a profounder possession. Names, after all, are words; but living animals are words made flesh. If you can put your hand upon the actual warm body, the breath-indwelt being itself, you "know" this being with a piercing closeness only less than if you had created it. You "take" it as, I suppose, a hunter thinks to take the creature he kills and so makes his; but after you have taken it, it remains alive and free and still warm with breath.

I touched my coon now. He made no objection, but only ducked his black-masked head a little and continued to clutch my knee. His thick coarse fur, over his fat little side, was rough to the touch.

I felt in my jacket pocket and produced a remnant of chocolate bar.

The coon took it gravely in his fingers and turned it over three or four times, peering at it and picking at the shreds of foil. Then he stuffed it into his mouth, but not chewing or swallowing, wheeled around, and went trundling off earnestly on his interrupted journey toward the brook.

He had in mind, no doubt, to wash his gift before eating it. Our coons wash almost everything, at least if they are anywhere near water at the time. All the brook foods they take —frogs, crayfish, water beetles, larvae of aquatic insects, even the occasional minnow that nimble coon fingers may manage to clutch—are all solemnly dipped and soused in the water from which they have just been extracted before our little bears eat them.

Mary and I have had many nighttime meetings with our raccoon neighbors and have come to know them well. It is partly because a raccoon has this mixture of bland spirit and high curiosity, which may move him to put his paws gravely on the knee of a strange naturalist looming suddenly in the dark, and it is partly because a raccoon is virtually always hungry. Raccoon is an Indian name; it means "he who scratches with his hands." Our little bear goes hand-scratching, all through the dark hours, in a limitless interest in finding something to eat. This hunger brings him to our brook, to the bird feeder, up into the maple tree outside Mary's window—to innumerable places where he is easy to find and watch.

Perhaps there are such things as thin raccoons, but Mary and I have not seen one. Ours stuff themselves prodigiously. If a coon padding along our brook cannot paw out crayfish, he happily paws out polliwogs, snails, or almost any other small creature discoverable in the flowing water. If he is minded to hunt the stream edge rather than the water itself, he is delighted to dine on turtle eggs scooped out of their shallow cavities in the damp sandy soil; or, going further into the field, he is pleased to pounce on grasshoppers and crickets in the grass. Coons hunt for birds' nests on the ground, for field mice in their hummocked runways, for nearly any small life astir in the darkness. They are not exclusively hungry for a meat diet, nor even primarily so. A very large grizzle-furred coon, one night when Mary and I were sitting in our woods-edge garden, came clambering up on our small grape arbor (a somewhat misleading and pretentious term, this; it is just twenty feet or so of old fence with a gnarled grapevine growing over it) and stayed there happily until we went to bed, stuffing himself with the small sour fruits. Coons eat cherries, pokeweed berries, pears, almost any fruit, wild or domesticated. It is an omnivorousness valuable to coons, for our little bears do not hibernate. They are abroad in our neighborhood in all but the fiercest winter weather. Their enthusiasm for eating almost anything at all makes food-securing relatively easy even when our woods and fields lie snow-blanketed; and when a coon does retire to its den to doze away a few weeks of exceptionally bitter weather, it is plump enough to live happily on its own fat until it feels like venturing out again to go padding forth through our countryside on fresh explorations, leaving its barefoot-child's paw-prints in the snow.

Being so everlastingly and miscellaneously hungry, and in our piece of the world so unafraid, raccoons have come into Mary's and my life and night-observings in a continually neighborly way and have given us a chance to find out curious things about them.

161

There are their climbing skills, for instance. It is prodigious that such fat little bears as these can perform such arboreal maneuvers as we have seen them carry out. It is not only prodigious, but puzzling. There is an endless supply of ground edibles for coons. But every now and then a coon takes a notion it must have a bird's egg—or possibly even make a try for a sleeping bird roosting in the darkness of the high branches—and it swarms aloft as nimbly as a squirrel. There have been two occasions particularly when Mary and I have been astonished by our heavy-bodied coon neighbors' climbing.

There is a big sugar maple just outside the west bedroom window of our old house. One or two of its outermost branch tips brush the window screen. Over the years, a great many pairs of small eyes have gleamed in at us in the darkness from the leafy branch tips or from the screen itself: the tiny blazing eyes of summer moths glittering with reflection; the bright little eyes of a brown bat, hooking its thumbs to the screening, resting, and looking in; the big night-shining eyes of a White-foot, venturing out on the twig tips to harvest maple seeds. One October night a few years ago, while I was still in my study downstairs, there came an urgent call from Mary to come have a look at this upstairs western window. We were being looked in at, improbably, by a raccoon. He had tightroped his way far out on a limb almost to its slender tip, and then with a trapeze swing had flung himself out and gripped the window screen with his fingers. Now he was hanging and swaying, looking into the room in mild and solemn coon inquiry. As I took a few steps toward the window, his forepaws dropped from the screen, he swung in a wild tumbling arc, and then in an instant he was miraculously right-side-up again on the limb, padding unhurriedly back along it toward the tree trunk. A few minutes later we could hear him, down below in the darkness, scratching and scrabbling his way toward earth again.

The other coon climb was on a night up by Owl Rock, when we lay on our backs in the crackling field grass of hot August and watched the sky for meteoric showers. There is a big dead, or almost dead, beech tree there, and the black ruin of its spire stretched up against the vault of night-blue sky we were watching.

Suddenly Mary broke the starry stillness with a whisper. "Isn't that something moving up there, about two-thirds of the way toward the top?"

It was. It was a raccoon.

On and up he climbed, up, up, up the swaying rotted shell of trunk until he was nearly to the pinnacle. He must have been thirty feet or more from earth. We had already guessed what his goal might be, and now he let us see that it was. That spring a pair of sparrow hawks had nested in an old flicker hole almost at the treetop. Perhaps our coon had found eggs in that nest, and the memory had remained obscurely in his coon-consciousness, or perhaps his climb now was just a chance exploration. At any rate he reached the hole, halted

163

there a moment as if taking a firm grip on the teetering trunk, and then cautiously reached an arm inside the hole. He stayed thus for several minutes, feeling around inside the deep cavity with his agile and sensitive little hand; and then he slowly drew forth his paw, empty, and looked at it. We must have seen coons make this gesture scores of times; but our delight in it never lessens. It is such a foolish little gesture, so serious, so solemn. Presently, convinced that he had in fact achieved a haul of Nothing, the coon began the long course of backing bear-fashion down the great beech trunk, and in a few minutes dropped into the underbrush and went patter-padding off into the night.

Knowing our neighbors the coons has involved few more surprising discoveries for Mary and me than in the matter of their voices. We are always thinking that we know all the sounds of nighttime outdoors after so many years of listening and watching in the dark hours; and we are always hearing new voices; and then they are always turning out to be the commentaries of ring-tailed little brothers of the bear.

The commonest sound our coons make, when the moon comes up over the dark woods, is a querulous kind of little gruntlike murmuring—what is usually called their "churring," though to Mary and me it seems to have a quality that, when I wrote it out a few pages ago in telling about the chocolate-bar coon, I tried to catch by spelling it *oonk-oonk-oonk*. This is the sound our coons make most familiarly when they are prowling along the brook edge or sniffing and pattering around our woodshed, feeling pleased, gently inquisitive, and characteristically hungry. But when our ring-tailed neighbors are hunting intently, or when a whole family is prowling the neighborhood in a troop, they sometimes give voice to a *hoo-loo-looing* that sounds like screech owls. This long-drawn tremolo carries considerable distances through our dark woods. Alone in a tree fork, feeling drowsily fat and serene, a raccoon sometimes chirps and twitters to himself in a little private music almost like a songbird. When coons dispute amongst themselves, a kind of yapping growl, with squealings and whickerings intermixed, occasionally comes from them. Once two coons by our brook, under the little willow that the heifers have rubbed bare of all its lower branches, debated so loudly in these squealy growls that they woke us. Learning to know the many sounds of coon-comment is a kind of neighborly intimate knowledge, of course, that Mary and I love to gather; but our gathering still remains a long way from finished. Our little bears, as they go prowling around at their coony trundle through the darkness, have more kinds of things to say, I am pretty sure, than we have even yet found out.

For all the coons we meet in night encounters, chances to see a ring-tailed neighbor in daylight don't come along. So on the summer afternoon up the wood road, when the bit of suet disappeared into the oak hollow and a black-masked face peered out at us, we forgot about heat, midges, and all other considerations, and gave ourselves over to peering back.

On the opposite side of the wood road from the oak tree from which our coon was looking out, there is a steep bank overgrown with maple saplings. We subsided on this in immediate immobility. If the dark eyes in the black-masked little face watched us at all, they did so in no alarm and with only the mildest curiosity. Having fetched in the bit of suet from its doorway, the coon seemed to have exhausted all energies available to a night-loving, dampness-loving spirit in the hot sunlight of a summer afternoon. Our coon looked out upon the woods world, and us, in a dozy inattention.

Mary and I sat still, I suppose, for a quarter of an hour, while mosquitoes fed on us and the thrushes sang their chiming notes in the woods's stillness.

"I think," I said, "we might as well go home. It looks to me as though this coon is asleep."

So it was. The small pointed chin had for some minutes been slowly sagging lower and lower, and now it rested on the sill of the oak-hollow doorway. The coon's dark eyes had closed. Our black-masked little neighbor, while two naturalists stared intently from only a few yards away, had subsided into the deeps of whatever raccoons may dream about.

We got up, not being particularly quiet about it, and started down the wood road for home. Looking back as we walked away, we could see that not even one eye opened to watch our going.

In early evening, we were off up the wood road again. As dusk came on, we thought, our coon would wake up and go prowling off to explore the night, and we wanted to see this.

There was no coon dozing in the oak hollow. We must have delayed our evening visit a little too late, and our coon was already away to the brook to paddle in the mud and feel around for edibles.

We turned to start home, adventureless.

Just then, in the quiet dusk, we heard a small muffled rumpus. There were some faint thumps and scrabblings and a kind of breathy little squealy noise; and all this was coming, unmistakably, from down inside the hollow oak. We looked at each other and sat down instantly among the maple saplings.

In a minute, a coon face popped into view in the oak-tree doorway. If Mary and I had been quiet before, we were now as still as any of the mossy stones on the bank where we sat. For the quizzical little coon face peeping out from the oak hollow was not the face of the grown-up coon we had watched lazing and dozing in the afternoon. This was a baby. Our oak-tree hollow was a coon-family house.

A second little black-masked face peeked up over the rim of the doorway, then a third, then a fourth. A quartet of little bears, standing tiptoe in the house where they must have been born less than two months before, probably in May, peered out solemnly upon the evening woods. They nudged and jostled one another, eager for a better look at things; and presently a furry little hind leg, with a barefoot-baby's sole,

167

was hiked up over the doorsill and one of the youngsters came clambering out backwards.

Adult raccoons can come down a tree either backwards in bear-fashion, or headfirst like a descending squirrel. They must become confident enough to try headfirst descents, however, only after a good deal of experience; for now as a second coonlet followed the first one out of the hollow, and then the third and fourth came after, each carefully turned around backwards on the threshold. The descent of the oak was a slow affair of much slipping and scrabbling, with little black-masked faces turning again and again to look downward. When the last baby was nearly to earth, the face of the big coon, their mother, appeared in the doorway and peered down at them. She slipped over the doorsill in a quick ripple of confident motion and came down the rough bark almost at a scamper.

The coon family stayed within our range of vision for perhaps ten minutes. To Mary and me, unmoving on the maple-shadowed bank, it seemed much longer. Nearly all our most intimate adventures in participating in the lives of our animal neighbors have had this deceptive time quality. Partly, I suppose, it is because time is experience. When a deeply meaningful thing happens to you, there is an adventure in experience so large that it seems as though the time period to hold it must be big too. But there is also the fact that animals, and particularly youngsters bursting with the initial excitement of being alive and aware, can crowd a tumult of activities into a few minutes. While we watched our coon family, they gradually worked their way from the oak tree down toward the little brook that flows through the bottom of the ravine. This is a distance of perhaps twenty yards. But, in covering it, the coonlets made uncountable detours and side excursions, scratching away at the base of an old cedar stump, pawing up, fascinated, dead leaves and pine needles and the dark woods loam, sniffing and snuffing. Every now and then, we could see, the youngsters found something to eat, but we couldn't make out what it was. Twice, as they trundled along, two of them paused to grapple together in a ferociously playful tussle. Standing up like bears, they did not snap or bite at each other, but simply held their mouths wide open and made enthusiastic lunging pretenses. Neither of them, all the while, made a sound.

At the edge of the brook the coon family paused briefly and investigated the water. This brook, unlike the main brook that runs through our acres, is only a wet-weather stream. There are no fish in it, and relatively few other aquatic creatures, because of its way of drying up, except for some rocky pools in the hemlock woods higher on the hill, whenever there is a period of drought. Mother raccoon and her youngsters paddled in it only a minute or two, the babies picking up their paws and then plunging them down in the water again in the absorbed kneading motion coons so often use, and then mother coon mounted a dead pine trunk that lies fallen across the stream. The babies scrambled up after her, and the whole

169

family crossed this natural bridge in single file and disappeared at their rolling coon-trundle in the dark undergrowth beyond. It was the last we saw of them that night.

Mary and I had coon-family evenings all summer and into the autumn.

We would go up the wood road a little after eight o'clock, just as twilight starts fading toward darkness and the first hawk moths come hovering around our garden in the dusk. Sometimes, after we had sat quiet for half an hour or so in the heavy shadow of our maple copse, watching the oak hollow, and had seen no stir of life, we would conclude that our coons had gone exploring for the night, and that it would be useless to wait for them to come home. The wood road in evening, even when coonless, however, is a place we love—with whippoorwills calling, and the damp evening smell of leaf mold and pines and brook-wet stones, and gliding owl shadows— so we never minded. On other evenings we would be in time to see the coon jaunt getting under way, and to learn some new small thing to increase our intimacy with coons.

We found out, after a while, what it was that the young coons so regularly and easily found to eat as they made their preliminary reconnoiter around the oak tree's base. It was earthworms. We also found out how very early in life a young coon learns, from following his mother, to adopt the all-around-every-which-way course of traveling which gives adult coons such success in eluding pursuers. A coon, as I was saying, has teeth big enough and claws powerful enough to make him a formidable adversary even for a large dog. The tales that tell of a coon drawing a pursuing dog into water and then tackling the dog and holding its head under water until it drowns, are sometimes true. But the bear's ring-tailed small brother fights only if it is unavoidable. (Shake a sapling with a treed coon in it, and even under this assault it is a rare coon that does not preserve, even while hanging on for life, a mild mood of mere startled curiosity, peeping out from the leaves continually to see what on earth is going on.) A coon's chief means of safety lies in elusion, and an old coon develops innumerable guiles and tricks of the trail: crossing and recrossing watercourses, climbing up one tree and down the next, trundling around this way and that in a crafty maze through the woods. Mary and I loved to watch the four young coons, first because they were following their mother and then later just because it had quickly become second nature to them, clambering up a stump and down the other side, crossing the brook on the pine trunk and then immediately crossing back by hopping boulders a few yards upstream. All this, now, was only play to them, but it was the start of a life way that would be habit-fixed. In dangerous times they would be able to call on it and turn it into one of the most useful woodscunnings possessed by any of our animal neighbors.

Occasionally, as summer passed into fall, I would go up the wood road at noontime to have a look at our house of coons.

The youngsters, now grown to perhaps five pounds or so,

were never visible. They were undoubtedly sound asleep deep in the oak hollow. But several times I was able to see their mother, stretched out sun-dozing on a broken-off dead branch.

Familiar as Mary and I are with every tree contour and branch pattern, up along this woods trail of ours, I doubt if I should have seen her if I had not known of the oak hollow's tenancy and so made a point of walking all around the tree in a wide circle. The branch on which the mother raccoon did her sunning was nearly invisible from the wood road. She would lie stretched flat and limp along it, her hind feet tucked under her on the branch, her forepaws dangling, her little pointed chin pressed against the sun-warmed bark. On these noonday visits I made no attempt at quietness, but walked briskly through the crackling dead leaves and whipping underbrush. Soaked in sun and sleep, the raccoon mother never stirred or opened her eyes.

One day while I stood watching her, rapt in her little-bear repose, a crow saw her too. *Caw!* went the alarm signal ringing through the autumn woods; and *Caw!* came an answer from over beyond the ridge. Within minutes a clamoring company of crows had gathered in hubbub. In an uproar of excitement they swooped around the oak tree, diving down in furious flights within a foot or two of the branch where the sleeper lay, coming so close to touching her that I could see her thick gray fur riffled by the passage of their wings, and making their strident tumult. Two berry-dark eyes opened briefly, in a black-masked little face, and considered all this. Gently they closed again and stayed closed.

Young coons stay with their mother a long while, usually into the winter, so Mary and I expected many continuing weeks of intimacy with our house of coons. But toward mid-October we went up the wood road to our coon tree several evenings in a row without seeing any of the family about. A few days later, on a noontime visit, I found a definitive sign that our family of ring-tailed neighbors had left us. Across the opening of the oak hollow a spider web had been spun.

The oak hollow, I should guess, had turned out to be too small for the present size of the family, and they had moved off to a larger house. We never found it. Perhaps some of the coons we met here and there in the smoky apple-scented twilights that autumn were members of the family, but we could not know.

"Hoo-loo-loo-loo!" drifts a faint far-off tremolo through our darkness and comes in at our windows.

"Bears," smiles Mary happily, in tribute to James Fenimore Cooper and an ignoring of the strictness of taxonomy.

"Hoo-loo-loo-loo!" it comes again; and we have a picture in our minds of earnest little black-masked figures trundling along the brook in the moonlight, dipping their monkeylike paws in the muddy shallows, sousing and swashing and scrubbing.

Bears, monkeys, or just raccoons, those that scratch with their hands, we like having them around us for neighbors.

Cottontail Companions

Quietly, quickly, in the spring night, a female rabbit digs and scrabbles among the tall stems of meadow grass. As she excavates the shallow earth depression, her soft pivotal ears, warm and delicate as a deer mouse's, turn this way and that and listen: owl hoot, fox yap, the patter of a weasel, all distant, none menacingly close.

She paws the night-cool earth until the cavity is five or six inches deep. It is perhaps the third she has dug.

A week earlier, in the May darkness, she may have dug a hollow in our sidehill corn lot, and then, in the rabbit way,

174

have hidden in a nearby blackberry tangle and watched it. Possibly it was found by a fox; and she ran scuttering and zigzagging through the darkness, and that nest site was abandoned. The second cavity which she dug and watched may have been in too low-lying land; a shower filled it with rain water. Now she has dug this third, among the tall grass stems, and has watched it and seen no harm come to it, and the fetal babies are kicking imperatively in her womb.

She crouches in the earth cavity and turns around and around, shaping and modeling, as does a nest-building bird. With dry leaves and withered grasses she makes a lining, and then plucks out tufts of the soft thick fur from her breast and sides and pats them into place to make a furry cup, and finally pulls into place a covering of weed stalks and dried leaves to make a roof.

She grows quiet now in the darkness, listening to the night sounds of bats and distant owls and stridulous crickets, breathing the night exhalations from the furrowed farm fields and the leafing woods of spring.

There issue from her presently, as several times each year, the three to seven blind and helpless squirming babies which will shortly be ready—quickly maturing like all much-preyed-on things—for adulthood as a new generation of soft-footed, wary-treaded, gentle-hearted browsers among our meadow grass and nibblers of mushroom caps under the moon.

Family rearing is one of the three primary rites of rabbit

life, as well as in all other natural lives. Second is the securing of food, which for rabbits means only the cropping of all kinds of green shoots and in winter the gnawing of the buds and bark of saplings; and third is the maintenance against enemies. Weasels, foxes, dawn-flying hawks—the woods and fields and sky are populous with hunters of rabbits. In the heart of a rabbit, as in the hearts of all wild things, there is no continuum of terror; there is no long sick dread, for forgetfulness and concern with immediacy are of the essential nature of animal mind. But our cottontail is wary, alert, with a protective timidity in its blood such as even far more formidable wild animals, indeed wolves, natively have; and the young rabbits have not been long out of the nest before they begin acquiring the protective lore which their instinct bids them accumulate: the finding of every hollow stump, every abandoned woodchuck burrow, every tumbled and intersticed old stone fence within this area of countryside, and the storing in their dim little animal memories of the geography of these sanctuaries.

Rabbits must maintain themselves against their enemies mostly by cunning flight and hiding. Only rarely is there an exception. It comes, when it does, in the nesting period, when, in the darkness, a mother rabbit, her small warm wriggling brood beneath her, catches the sound of a nearby twig snapping under a stealthy tread and smells the rank odor of a fox. A kind of wild valiance may then leap up in her gentle blood. She may spring, in the darkness, straight for the intruder, her long hind legs flying in a "rabbit kick," her soft ears laid back against her skull. By the surprise of her assault she may drive off her enemy. Or there may pierce the darkness, in a moment, the long high scream which sends every other rabbit in nearby woods and meadows scuttling to cover. They know what it is. It is a rabbit's death cry.

To doze by day, sniffing the smell of sun-warmed earth and dreaming obscure animal dreams in a "form" of leaves and grasses; to hop forth in the dusk, soft-eyed, alert-eared and browse tranquilly among the damp green shoots in the moonlight; to zigzag and backtrack and hide in chosen sanctuaries to escape from enemies; to drink at small forest pools; to raise broods of soft-nosed little ones in fur-lined nests; to frisk and rush and leap and caper sometimes in antical frolics which are the exultancy of the wild heart in the fact of aliveness and the sweetness of the primordial world—that is the whole story of rabbits.

It is not much of a story. Perhaps not. But Mary and I have loved to construct it, over the years, from a multitude of quiet observations of these small cotton-tailed neighbors of ours and from adventures into intimate participation in their lives. Rabbits, perhaps more than almost any other animals, are meaningful to nearly all of us from childhood; for we meet them very early in stories and picture books. Those of us who are already disposed in childhood to be naturalists also meet and come to know living rabbits as very likely the first and most familiar animal neighbors of our countryside.

Rabbits browsed and scampered and twitched their noses in the green Irish fields where a small Mary went exploring, in her first spellbound discoveries of the outdoors. In her memory they go with the sea mists, the old stone walls with roses growing over them, and the whitewashed cottages with turf smoke curling from their chimneys. In my own memory, cottontails are associated with nearly every boyhood woods prowl and field excursion—the startling *pouf!* of a cottontail jumping from almost under foot and bounding zigzag across a hot summer field where I was searching for meadow-lark nests, the gentle nearness of a cottontail nibbling the evening grass close by me as I hid in a garden in the summer dusk and waited for sphinx moths to come to the glimmering white phlox blossoms, the tracks of cottontails patterning the fresh snow when I set off through winter woods on crackling mornings to look for promethea cocoons and pine grosbeaks. Old World rabbits or American cottontails, these small, soft-eared neighbors go back in Mary's memory and mine as far as we can recollect. It is partly, I suppose, on this account that we have peculiarly loved the intimate neighborliness of rabbits in our hundred-odd-acre world. They are very old friends of ours, going back all the way to the designs on our nursery wallpaper and to childhood's first enchanted glimpses of the companioning creaturely outdoors.

We have a good many cottontail neighbors in our woods and fields. Finding a house of cottontails is not so uncommon

an adventure as finding a house of coons (though I should
insist that in its quiet way it is as much an adventure), and
baby rabbits are a good deal easier to see than little fawns.
Though Maytime is the season Mary and I think of as particularly rabbits' family-period, for May and June are the
great birth months of our outdoor year and it is then that we
specially go looking for nests, our cottontails breed and raise
babies during nearly seven months of the twelve. Only from
about September to about January is there a pause in the
enormous fecundity of our rabbits. A cottontail can give birth
to babies before she is a year old. Her period of gestation is
only about a month, and she averages perhaps four or five
babies to a litter. A mathematics-minded naturalist once
computed, if I remember the figures right, that one pair of
cottontails, if their youngsters and their youngsters' youngsters all survived for a period of five years, would become a
cottontail throng of something over three hundred thousand.
So Mary and I have cottontails companioning us despite all
the enormous preying upon them by nearly every predatory
creature on our patch of earth. The owls glide down in the
dusk and take rabbits. The hawks coursing over our fields
take rabbits. The big blacksnake that lives under the spring-
cover up on our sidehill slithers through the high grass and
seeks out rabbit nests. Everywhere in our woods and pastures
there are natural rabbit-catchers, swooping on silent wings,
gliding silently on snake-scaled bellies, padding on silent
paws. Against this, cottontails oppose the resistance of their

numbers; and it is a sufficiently triumphal resistance, in its gentle rabbit way, so that every year we have a surplus of cottontails surviving to browse on our dew-wet pasture grass under the summer moons and nibble birch twigs up along the old wood road when the snow lies deep.

Of all the details of cottontail life that Mary and I have liked finding out, in our neighborly acquaintance with these soft-furred fellow beings of ours that live out their little rabbit lives against such odds, I think perhaps it is their nest life that has most beguiled us. It is, after all, the very center and strength of rabbitdom. A cottontail has only moderately long legs, not tremendous jumping legs like a jack rabbit. It can sometimes get away from an enemy in a short sprint; it cannot win in a long pull. It is not usually expert in complicated trail strategies. A chased cottontail mostly relies on zigzagging and on occasional side leaps and seldom practices much more crafty means of escape. Where cottontails win their way to survival, exactly speaking, is in their nursery. About one litter of cottontails in three, I think, survives to the point where the baby rabbits are able to leave the nest. Mary and I look into cottontails' babyhood and feel we are at the heart of the secret strength of these twinkle-nosed small neighbors of ours.

Cottontails make their nests in all sorts of places. Most often, we have found them in our open fields or meadows, frequently in the thin-soiled rocky fields on the slope of the hill; but we have also come upon nests at the edge of old stone walls in the hedgerow thickets, in the middle of an alder clump not far from the Muskrat Pool, and, once, under an arching root of a big oak tree deep in the woods. A mother cottontail is a strong digger and can send the earth flying almost as fast as a woodchuck; but in selecting her nest site she is likely to choose a place where there is already the beginning of a cavity or cranny. Of all the cottontail nests Mary and I have found, the one that we were able to watch most closely and that gave us our fullest opportunity to add details to our knowing of cottontails' nursery life was built in a sidehill depression formed when a small boulder had been dislodged by the runoff of spring rains. This nest was on the abrupt slope, overgrown with maple saplings and briers, that rises back of our old house beyond the edge of the garden. I found the nest by very nearly sitting on it.

I climb this back-of-the-garden hill a good deal just to sit in the hot sun and smell the sun-baked leaves and earth and stare out over the Catskills. A neighborhood naturalist like me finds his most intense pleasures in intimately close knowledge: in the close-up, the little view, the animals that are so immediately his neighbors he can put his hand on them. But occasionally it is good too, for proportion, to see also—at least with the eye of your mind—the huge far-stretching rest of the world beyond; and the best way for me to do this is by climbing part way up a hill and looking out.

Our valley lies winding away below me—old farmhouses and red barns, checkered hayfields and corn lots and rolling pasture, the shining line of the brook as it twists its way down the valley with willows along its borders. Over beyond this valley, and the next and the next, lies the river; and beyond that are the curves and peaks of the blue hills. Mary's and my small world is the kind of world we want, a world in little and in intimacy; but the immenseness of Out There wants remembering. In the blue hills at which I can look there are bears. We have none in our neighborhood; but it is good to look out and remember them. On that rounded Catskill mountaintop, which I can just make out against the haze of the summer sky, there are porcupines clambering in their slow way around the treetops. Over beyond those hills —well, over beyond those hills stretches the creation on and on and on, teeming with creaturely lives. It is a good expansion for me, to be thinking of it. Not that Mary or I, to be sure, ever loses sight of the enormousness of animal life. It is because we know it so well, after all, that we have taken a sample world for ours. Still, looking out from the hillside over the winding valley and the far mountains, awareness does open up in a special way. You can almost *see,* as it were, expansed before you, the immenseness of the great family of fellow lives; and it makes for a specially compelling realization.

It was a hot June afternoon on the hillside, and I had climbed up there and was sitting, lost in these great distances.

We human beings are one of a gigantic company, and on

this afternoon I could "see" it: a company comprising innumerable species that fed and bred and lolled in the sunlight aeons before our coming, innumerable other species that, not impossibly, may (depending on what turns our planet's natural history takes) be continuing to exist through an infinity of recurring similar cycles long after mankind has sizzled or frozen into nothing; and still other innumerable species which even now, at this moment, are engaged in the process of life rituals closely akin to our own, but in myriads and multi-myriads which dwarf our own dimensions, in the physical terms of specieshood, at least, nearly to negligibility. While men are breathing and breeding and struggling with their problems and presently dying, so are some four thousand other species of kindredly warm-blooded mammals. So are considerably more than a million separate and distinct species of insects, making up a total insectdom whose aggregate individuals could not be numbered in our mathematics. Perhaps two million of the beings called men died in the last war. The being called a bacterium is also, in its fashion, an individual and a life; and two million such micrococci might live out their intricate and eventful life cycles on one man's forefinger. It is not necessary to think of the dramatically tiny forms of microphytic beings to be overwhelmed by realization of the huge companionship, the gigantic dance of life, in which we are caught up as only one participant. We dance the life dance in company with fifteen thousand types of spiders. We are a part of a fellowship that embraces at least two thousand varieties of snakes. This green and flowering earth of ours may be man's for dominion, but there flies around our heads a cloud of fifteen thousand varieties of birds. Over the Catskills, almost I could hear the rush of their wings.

It may humble us to think of it. We are one small ingredient in a whole of unimaginable vastness. More, we are a part of a general and embracing interdependence. We are here at all because there is a woven relationship, so intricately threaded that the whole pattern of the weave is beyond our understanding, between ourselves and birds, between birds and vegetation, between mammals and fish, between suns and seeds, between every ingredient of the totality and every other ingredient. We are in no sense something alone and independent. We are supported by starfish. An owl props us. Earthworms minister to hold us upright. In certain Christian churches there is a difficult doctrine of interpenetration and interdependence which is called the doctrine of the mystical body of Christ. A naturalist must subscribe to a doctrine in biological idiom that is not less stupefying: the body entity of all of nature and our dependent membership in it. The doctrine is indisputable; and to grasp it has this result: that no creature of our earth, no life on it, seems any longer negligible or any longer alien. It is a part of us, and we of it. We partake in a common being. If we slaughter a bird, we injure, in a sense much more than merely mystical, the tissue of ourselves. When we regard a toad or a snail, we are regarding a part of our own total selves. We are not a lone thing, huge

and isolated. We are a very small thing, precarious with creaturely dependence. We may not despise, any more than we
may despise a brother or an organ of our own body, even a
being so small, so dim, so remote from us, as, say, this common grasshopper rustling in the grass here beside me on the
hot sidehill under the June sun.

I looked down beside me to see the grasshopper, who had
been rustling and crackling invisibly for several minutes,
plucking my thoughts gradually back from their large June-
drugged wanderings into zoological infinity. I could not see
him. I began idly parting grass-blades and blackberry shoots
with my fingers; and then suddenly I was brought back
sharply and entirely to here and now and was home again,
a neighborhood naturalist with animal neighbors literally
under his hand. Less than a foot from where I had sat down,
and concealed by a little arch of withered grass that bowered
a hollow where a stone had rested, lay a huddle of five baby
cottontails.

As the sunlight struck them, when I parted the concealing
grass, they squirmed together in a tight little cluster.

They could not have been more than hours old. I think
they had been born the previous night in the warm June
darkness. The other cottontail babies Mary and I have found
have had at least a faint shadowing of fur on their blunt-
headed little bodies. These were as naked as newly hatched
baby robins. As a matter of fact, in their almost formlessness
and the bluish-pink crinkle of their infant skin, they might

almost have been taken at a hasty glance for a nestful of baby birds.

I brushed grass strands back over them and stood up quickly. Mary must see this, and immediately. I broke the top of a little nearby maple sapling to mark the place (the sidehill is all one uniform scraggle, and to walk back and forth over it, searching, would be to risk stepping on the tiny family) and came down the hill to summon her.

We spent perhaps an hour of the late afternoon that day just sitting quietly on the sidehill, a yard or two from our cottontail nest, taking an occasional peek into this handful of warm, pink little lives, talking together and watching the hills and being happy. No matter how long you have been animalizing (a useful word from an old farmer over across our hill for the kind of thing neighborhood naturalists love to do), there is an undiminishing delight in occasions like this. An infant rabbit, hours old, is miraculous; and there is no need to feel ashamed in saying so. The tiny pink bodies, huddling together, were only babies of one of the most familiar and unspectacular animals that live with us here on this piece of earth; but even the most primary philosophy or poetry must find them as big with wonder as a new sunrise, as strange as a star. We had a wonderful time.

It was unnecessary to worry whether we might be keeping the mother cottontail from her nursing. Even when their babies are quite tiny, our cottontails don't come to the nest to feed them during the daylight hours. What a mother rabbit does, as a rule, is make herself a small "form" in the grass some distance from the nest, from which she can keep an eye on it as she did when she was selecting the nest site and testing it for safety, and from which she can hear any squeal of alarm from her youngsters. She comes to the nest to feed them only after sunset. While Mary and I sat on the sunlit sidehill, talking and watching and "thinking ourselves into" our grass-arched nest of rabbits, the mother was probably hidden within sound of our voices. But though a cottontail deserts her nest readily before her babies are born, there is little danger that she will abandon it when it holds youngsters. The maternal instinct in most of our animal neighbors (and in birds, for that matter) builds in slow crescendo after mating time. It intensifies to passion with the coming of the young. Likely enough, the alert ears of a mother rabbit were listening to us, and perhaps even watchful cottontail eyes—those soft, dark, wary eyes so convexly designed that a rabbit has virtually full-circle vision—were peering at us from green hiding nearby; but after all we were only a pair of naturalists, not something to be fled or fought.

I suppose "fought" may seem a curious word to be using. But cottontails, mild little neighbors of ours as they are, have their valiance. I was saying that a mother cottontail, in a flare of spirit, may fly at a marauding fox and drive him away from her babies. I used the particular instance of a fox because once, back in my boyhood when I was keeping a cottontail nest under observation with a view to taking one of the babies home when it had grown big enough, I saw such a rabbit-fox encounter and have never forgotten it. But a mother cottontail, I think, may fight almost any moderate-sized predator that comes to threaten her homestead. Certainly she often fights fellow rabbits. When she is carrying her babies and preparing for nest-making, she becomes hostile to her mate. She turns on him, fighting off his attentions, and presently bites and rabbit-kicks him until he has left the neighborhood. In family time she requires to be alone with her babies. Also, when she has a nest of youngsters, she is fiercely vigilant against the trespass of other female rabbits in the territory. Let a wandering female stray anywhere into this piece of field or woods and the mother cottontail is after her in a flying rush, chasing her in a furious pell-mell zigzag. A few summers ago a cottontail mother had a nest of babies over at our far pasture edge, in a hollow scooped out in what had been a cow's hoof-print. One evening Mary and I watched her pursuit of another rabbit who had come too close. She chased the intruder all the way to the birch copse, a distance, I should guess, of nearly fifty yards.

In the warm afternoon sidehill sun, Mary and I had our leisurely fill of rabbit baby-sitting. No sign of their mother turned up.

As the evening darkened toward night, we went up the slope again for another look. We approached the broken-topped maple sapling gently and cautiously this time, not wanting to startle the cottontail mother if she should be at home for a feeding; but she was not there. The moment we bent over the nest hollow, however, we knew that she had paid at least one visit tonight to her young ones. She had tucked them into bed.

This may sound a sentimental sort of thing to say. But in fact it is as precise a way as I know to describe what Mary and I have again and again seen happen in the nurseries of these animal neighbors of ours. When a mother cottontail has given her nurslings a feeding and is about to slip away again into the night to forage for herself, she pulls a covering of wisps of grass and fur over her little ones. It makes a thin blanket over them, at once a warmth against the chill of the dark hours and a concealment. When she comes back for the next feeding visit, she paws and nuzzles the protective blanket aside. Leaving once more, she spreads it in place again. In some rabbit nests Mary and I have found, the blanket amounts to little more than a sprinkling of material. In others it is matted and substantial. (As far as I have been able to discover, the warmth or frostiness of our weather has little, if anything, to do with it.) Over our nest of sidehill infant cottontails, there was now spread such a thick littering of dry grass and fur tufts that we could only just make out their little pink shapes, motionless in sleep, underneath. There had been no blanket over them in the afternoon. We bent over the little crib of cottontails for only a moment or two in the dusk, for at night the mother is likely to be very near, and then we came quietly and quickly down the hill.

Our Animal Neighbors

When Mary and I visited our cottontails the next morning—a morning of thin drizzle, cold for June, with robins, red-eyed vireos, and thrushes all singing their tumult of rain song from among the dripping trees as we climbed the hill—we found the babies heavily blanketed with the wet matted layer lying soggily on them. I poked it aside with a forefinger, and Mary and I looked at each other in surprise. Our almost unidentifiable little pink beings of the day before had turned into rabbits overnight.

They were still blunt-headed, lumpy and pinkish, and their little rabbit ears still lay flattened and shriveled, rather like the damp crumpled wings of a moth when it has just hatched from its cocoon. Their eyes, of course, were still sealed shut. They were still blind, deaf, helpless little mites of rabbits. But they were rabbits. They had begun to grow fur. They were only a day and a half or at most two days old, but already their vigorous little bodies—wriggling away from my finger strenuously as I touched the blanket—were shadowed with a perceptible fuzz. It behooves little cottontails to grow up fast. We had not realized, until this moment, just how fast.

Ours in the sidehill nest grew up completely in less than two weeks. We visited them every day or evening, sometimes both. On several evening visits we met the mother cottontail, moving in slow hops around the sidehill in the pale fading light of sunset, nibbling, eyeing us as we came climbing up. As we would approach the nest, she would usually huddle and hunch herself close to the ground and "freeze," always sideways to us as if paying us no attention, but watching our every move intently, of course, with her alert side vision. As long as we stayed by the nest, looking down at her growing babies, she would hold this taut immobility. The moment we left to start home, she would take several casual hops and resume her browsing. She never gave any greater evidence than this of being disturbed by our intimacy in the life of her family.

By the time the baby cottontails were a week old—give or take a day or so, since we had not seen them born—their eyes were open. Their crinkly little baby ears had perked up and become soft furry miniatures of their mother's, and now they could see and hear us when we climbed up for a look at them. At this stage in rabbit life, we have found by experience, young cottontails are likely to bolt from their nursery if anything frightens them severely, so Mary and I approached the nest by a long way around, coming toward it from the uphill side and approaching only just near enough to be able to see that the babies were still there. They looked altogether like rabbits now, warm-furred, with shy, alert eyes, ears cocked in sensitive listening. They had still not quite "grown up to their heads," and they still huddled in a compact little group in the nest; but they were examining the world and were beginning to entertain what glimmer of consciousness would light them through it, and they were lifting their small heads and twitching their noses.

When not quite two weeks had passed, we went to the cottontail nest one morning and found it empty.

Occasionally, when baby cottontails go hopping out into the green world for the first time, it is an act of abrupt severance from babyhood. This is especially likely to be the case if they leave the nest because something has alarmed them. Scuttering away in all directions, they are from that moment on their own; and they never come back to where they were born. More often, however, the babies leave home by a more gradual program; and this was the case with our sidehill family. When we went for a look at the nest late in the evening, the five small cottontails had all come hopping home to it and were gathered for the night in the familiar security.

The same thing happened the next day and the day after that: the nest only an empty little hollow when we visited it in daylight, and by late evening five small rabbits again in residence. During daytime the youngsters were scattered to hide in individual forms that they had learned now to make for themselves. Then, with dusk coming on, they forgathered. But the third night, even on our dusk visit, there were no cottontails. There were none even much later—nearly midnight—when, just to make sure, I went up the sidehill alone with a flashlight and turned the beam of it suddenly on the old nursery. The cottontail hollow had become only another little hollow in the grass with little to mark it as ever having been a rabbit house except a few bits of fur and matted grass left over from the tatters of the blanket. A rain or two, and a day or two, and there would be no sign at all. Our five little cottontails, which had been a family, were now permanently dispersed. They had mixed into the general population of our rabbit neighbors, who browse on the cool evening grass of our lawn, scamper and zigzag through the pastures and brier patches, and succumb in their hundreds to owl-pounce, snake-strike, and the snap of predatory jaws.

Rabbit deaths are all around us. In the night Mary raises up on an elbow, listens, and whispers "Hear that!" We know at once what it is—that thin, screaming squeal in the darkness. Something has caught a rabbit. We sit in a summer field and watch a marsh hawk coursing back and forth, back and forth, beating low over the tops of the tall grass on its rapid wings. Suddenly it drops and is on the ground for a moment, and then we see it rise laboring. It has a small cottontail struggling in its talons. *Yap-yap-yurrr!* The bark of a fox drifts to us through the moonlit woods. In a few minutes there is the long screaming; and we know that again a zigzagging running has not been enough, a motionless crouching in the underbrush with soft ears laid back and little rabbit muzzle pressed to little rabbit paws has not been enough.

Though rabbit deaths are so many around us, and cottontails' death squeals as familiar a sound in our night as the quaver of owls or the churring of frog-hunting coons, it does not seem to naturalists like us that this is dismaying. After all, we know our cottontails as neighbors; we have put our hands in the warmth of their small nests; we have seen them secure in the fulfillment of their little animal rounds; we know that they have their goods and excellences in the enjoyment of here and now; and if it is true, as it certainly is, that a mortally hurt doe cannot have her life gladness darkened by anticipating death, it is even surer that a cottontail reposes in the security of Now with no realizing outside that. There is always the matter too, for naturalists, of the Wholeness of this created world—the kind of far looking I was doing on the sunlit side-hill afternoon when I nearly sat on our new little rabbit family.

It is the essence of this sort of nature-mindedness to look upon the creation, in so far as is possible to a creaturely being like our human selves, with a long view, a wide view, a far view, trying to see the Wholeness of the thing. The larger and longer you can make your view this way, the more you can come to relegate the Whole's ingredients and particulars to their proper subordinate place and see them as only parts and portions within the greater pattern of the thrivingness of the Whole.

The death of a rabbit, looked at personally and isolatedly, may look like a tragedy. But if today there are rabbits capering and exuberating gladly in this neighborhood of Mary's and mine, it is because yesterday other rabbits died. Today's trees are thrusting upward and glorying in the sun because their roots are sunk in the bone dust of the trees of yesterday, which had their season and passed. The tide rises off South Africa; a throng of violets blooms in a New England meadow; a cottontail rabbit is caught by an owl up our old wood road; and all these events are caught together in the infinitely interwoven web of the Whole. Here is the living Whole shimmering and shining and thriving as it throve back in the dawn of creation when the morning stars sang together. Into its maintenance, to conserve it at each moment in the felicity of its repose in progress, go myriad interrelated factors. Some of them, seen in isolation, may seem hard for us to pronounce "good." It may seem hard to see any excuse for what this bloody-taloned owl has just done. It is easy to think that this or that creature of the creation is a "pest" and that we should be better off without it. We may fancy that, in our wisdom, we'd have arranged things differently. But the more nature-minded you become—the more long-viewed, the more disposed to see nature as a Whole and its parts in the light of that understanding—the more you come to accept and to rejoice in each and every of the particulars that go together to produce this general goodness of the walnut-sound and apple-sweet and life-exulting Whole.

These are the ponderous thoughts of naturalists, not rabbits. *They* know that this green world is excellent because they taste it so, feel it so in the play of their lithe muscles, sniff it so in the scents of clover blossoms and rain-wet apple twigs. Our cottontails squeal in the night. But they are happy companions to Mary and me, having their quiet little animal fulfillments all around us, and being no less delighted to savor the pungence of chickweed and goldenrod because (as they have not heard) the life span for a cottontail lasts at most only two or three years. Time is as long as you think it is; and rabbits think it is forever.

If cottontails succumb in hundreds to other animal neighbors of ours that prey on them, they also sometimes make extraordinary escapes. A cottontail lives in a little world, in physical dimensions as in awareness. A ten-acre piece of Mary's and my neighborhood may contain a cottontail's lifetime traveling. Some of the cottontails we have watched in intimacy near the house seem hardly to have ventured outside the immediate home acre. But a world, like time, is in a sense the size of what use you put it to; and a chased cottontail can do some wonderfully intricate running in one small orchard or pasture lot. It is no great strategist. It depends mostly on its hereditary technique of zigzag and side jump, and on the memory, stored in its subconscious, of the various obstacle-dodges, bolt holes, and brush piles it has located in its familiar feeding explorations of this small world. But occasionally it uses some variation, and Mary and I have seen at least two escapes that were extraordinary.

One May evening when we were sitting by the brook, a cottontail came tearing along the top of the old stone wall that retains the brook bank beside one of its deep pools. Close behind the rabbit, flowing and rippling along the wall like poured shadow, came a weasel. Suddenly the cottontail swerved and sprang in a side jump. Curving in a wide descending arc, it hurtled through the air and fell with a splash into the brook pool six or seven feet below, scattering startled trout, frogs, and water snakes, and sending ripples swashing up on the grassy banks. While the weasel crouched peering and weaving its narrow head in the oddly snakelike gesture these lean hunters have, the rabbit struck out, swimming. I don't know whether it was mere accident, or because the cottontail was confused, or just possibly because even a rabbit has a certain subliminal wild wisdom to give it the feel of a situation at a more primitive level than analytically understanding it, but at any rate the little fugitive in the water, instead of swimming across the pool, turned and headed off downstream. While Mary and I watched, a drenched little cottontail, looking like a bony, bedraggled muskrat, went flailing and dog-paddling down the watercourse, little ears sticking up preposterously above the dark swirling current. The cottontail paddled all the way to the farthest bend we could see, rounded it in a swirl and a swoosh down some small rapids there, and disappeared into the evening. We looked around for the weasel. The hunter was pattering back off up the wall in defeat.

Another time, in our orchard, one of our cottontails climbed a tree. This puts it a little fancifully but it may convey something of Mary's and my astonishment. We were in my workroom over in back of the old barn when it happened. A cottontail was being chased by one of the many marsh hawks which frequently sweep back and forth, in their low-flying vigilance, over our land. Repeatedly the hawk had dipped and veered, and repeatedly the cottontail had zigged and zagged and whisked under the rail fence and turned around again and got away. Old Dan and Frolic, the horses, keep the grass very short in the orchard. They spend a great deal of time, in the muggy days of fly season, under the gnarled old trees, some of which have branches just low enough to provide good back-rubbing. The orchard grass is cropped and trampled almost to bare earth, and the cover for a running rabbit is negligible. Mary and I were quite sure how this hawk-and-rabbit contest of endurance and agile swervings would end, with another small cottontail neighbor dispatched in contribution to the maintenance of that Whole which provides good life adventure for rabbits and marsh hawks alike. But it didn't end that way. Braking abruptly to a scudding stop and turn by an old apple-tree trunk, the cottontail released the muscle springs of his hind legs in a sudden prodigious hop, and in the next instant was sitting, demure as a little owl, in a fork of the trunk almost a yard above ground. The marsh hawk veered, banked, came back, but made no attempt to plunge into that bower for a strike. It beat back and forth uncertainly a few more times across the orchard, acting, we thought, as if completely at a loss to account for this impossible disappearance of its supper, and then it gave up and flew away.

The Old World rabbits that Mary knew in Wicklow lived in tunneled burrows under the green fields and along the hedgerows. The cottontails in our neighborhood don't do that.

For winter security, though, they do establish something almost like warrens; and these snow-mounded refuges are places Mary and I have loved to look into, deriving almost such a sense of intimacy from the experience as when we have been able to have a nestful of youngsters under our watch. A cottontail's paws are small and narrow, and they do not have any such "snowshoes" as make it possible for our less common neighbors, the varying hares, to walk over the top of fluffy drifts. A cottontail flounders and sinks in. Two or three times over the years, when I have gone struggling through our deep-drifted woods after long periods of heavy snow to see how our animal neighbors were making out, I have found the frozen bodies of little dead cottontails. No predatory animal had killed these, and it is unlikely they had died of starvation in a woodsful of pines, spruces, sumacs, sassafras, and a score of other trees and shrubs whose bark and twigs make good nibbling for wintering rabbits. They had just come to the end of their trails, apparently from exhaustion, trying to scrabble their way through the densely drifted snow. Most of our cottontail neighbors, when the winter weather is furiously severe, stay home. The shelter they love is a brush pile.

Mary and I have accumulated for our cottontails, in our many seasons of sharing this piece of earth with them, a brush pile big enough to give accommodation to dozens. Every time we pick up a dead branch or prune a tree or cut down a brier patch, we carry the litter to the same pile just within the woods edge beyond the garden. When the brush pile was still quite small, cottontail neighbors took to scratching their way into it in bad weather; and in later years, when it has become many yards across and several yards high, and has packed down to a massive density of twigs, our rabbits have made it into what amounts to a rabbit apartment house.

Except when a female has babies, cottontails are not contentious among themselves about territory. A throng of them can share equally a little piece. I don't know how many cottontails take refuge in our big brush pile in bitter weather, and I can't think of any way of finding out unless by the practical but impossibly unfriendly method of jumping up and down on the pile and counting the exodus; but it is surely a fine big company. Mary and I love to go to the brush pile on winter mornings after there has been a light fall of fresh snow during the night and see the evidence of a host of our cottontail companions, now dozing away the bright wintry daylight hours in the pile's sheltering security.

The tracks of their night excursions from the brush pile stretch out from it in dozens and dozens of radii—tracks leading off up the wood road, tracks going over to the sloping hayfield, tracks going down to the ice-sheathed brook, tracks coming back again to one or another of the small doorways that are all around the brush-pile's edge. Sometimes, as Mary and I stand in the snow, one of the inhabitants of the brushpile shelter pops out for a daylight excursion. We always take the opportunity to flop down on our stomachs and poke a flashlight into the chamber he has vacated and peer in. What makes naturalists be naturalists, no doubt, as I have suggested before, is partly a love of being animals ourselves; and if you can thrust your whole head and shoulders inside a rabbit house, and feel there the warmth of its just-vacated occupant, and see the little tufts of fur and the rabbit-nibbled twigs, you can plunge deeply into the reward of this transforming empathy and identification. The inside of a cottontail's winter house in our brush pile has almost smooth walls, with the twig ends bitten off nearly evenly. It is permeated with a faint little rabbity pungence like the smell of wet grass.

When Mary was a girl in Wicklow fields, she used to wish that, like Alice, she could somehow go down a rabbit hole. It used to seem to her that, if only she could slip through one of those entrances hidden in the hedgerow or close by the edge of the old stone wall, it would prove an entrance into an enchanted world. She would find out what rabbits were really like at home and be able to take close to her, as it were, hold in her hands, the rabbitness of things. In Mary's and my life together in our hundred-acre world with our cottontail companions, she says, she feels that she has been able in effect to slip through that magic door; and she thinks the enchantment has turned out to be not less than she had expected. A cottontail life is in a way a slight thing, brief and expendable. But when your own life and cottontail life are lived as close as neighbors—when you can put your finger on the felted blanket over cottontail babies, when you can have a rabbit come to you in the evening and take a carrot from your fingers, when you become familiar with the cry of rabbit death in the night and think about what it means, so tiny in itself and so big with consequence in the Wholeness which your mind expands to think about—when all your life becomes rabbit-close like this, the enchantment which for childhood must be expressed in a fairy tale comes into being in homely truth.

Our Fox Friends

If you live out in the country as Mary and I do, the maintenance of even a simple way of life requires a surprising number of chores. It is two-fifths of a mile from our old house to the dirt-road corner where the rural carrier deposits our mail; which means something like 250 miles of going and coming in the course of each year for fetching letters. Cow fences don't just stay up; they have to be continually mended and pieced, water fences particularly. No civil servant removes the garbage or the rubbish; the former must be toted up the side-hill to the distant woods edge, the latter toted over to an old silo foundation in an open field and burned. Bull thistles grow faster than pasture grass; they have to be kept down by hand. And so it goes.

The chores of country living could be a drudging monotony if they amounted only to the work or the walking. But for naturalists, of course, they always amount to more than that. An excursion up the sidehill, through the sun-hot blackberry tangles, is an opportunity not less promising for animal-adventuring just because you happen to be carrying the garbage. Bull thistles, if you come at them with a scythe in your hands, still have monarch butterflies or goldfinches on their broad pink flower tops. The road to the letter box is a woods-edge road and a brook-edge road and as good a place as any for finding out something new about one of our animal neighbors.

On a June evening I was walking along this road, returning home from the chore of depositing outgoing mail in the letter box for our rural postman to pick up in the morning. I was walking softly, of course. With naturalists it becomes a habit. Instinctively you avoid stepping on twigs or scuffing pebbles. Instinctively you are always watching and listening. The crunch and clatter of heavy walking not only spoils any chance of catching an animal neighbor unaware; it obliterates all the tiny and subtle sounds of which the "silence" of the outdoors is composed and which to a naturalist are meaningful and loved. For every loud woodchuck whistle or caroling vireo song there are a hundred small whispers and wisps of sound: the tiny lisping call of cedar waxwings, the little crackle of dead leaves as one of our garter snakes or "checkered adders" draws its length cautiously across them in the concealment of the undergrowth, the soft *chuk-tuk* of a mother grouse warning her chicks, or whatever. When Mary and I are walking or watching together, we spend hours without a syllable of conversation, but we are continually in communication, looking at each other, sharing the experience of the tiny bits of sound we hear together and interpret. Being a naturalist involves, as second nature, being quiet. Awareness grows in silence. As I say, I was walking softly along the homeward road, chewing a sassafras twig.

I was nearly within sight of our house when there came to me the sensation that I was being followed.

There may very well be faculties of supersensory perception. Massive evidence suggests there are. But my sensation of being followed, I think, perhaps came more probably through subconscious sensory perception. Within the limits of the sensory, as Mary and I are continually finding, we human beings have acuities scarcely suspected until we train them up by exercise and rescue them from their long drowse of disuse; and we have for years made a practice of doing this. After all, we were all animals not very long ago; and, as Mary and I feel about it, humanness should only expand, not supersede, the ancient animal-experiencing of things.

Once upon a time, according not only to the folklore and legends of all peoples but according also to the strict view of an anthropologist or biologist, we were altogether one of the animals. The creature Two Legs (to avoid argument over a more exact scientific name) was a completely creaturely creature, entirely a member of that general community of creatures which includes also raccoons, hawks, amoebas, lizards, and all the rest of the winged, furred, shelled, and scaly things that pursue the rounds of their animal destiny under the life-giving sun.

Two Legs stretched himself on a sun-warmed rock and basked in an animal beatitude like his brotherly woodchuck. He came prowling out of his den at sunup and snuffed the scents on the morning air like a fox. He ran when he smelled the danger-smell of an enemy; he capered and exulted when he experienced the good taste of food; he responded with animal enthusiasm and acquiescence to the urgency of sex, of sleep, of playfulness, and possibly, in the view at any rate of Metchnikoff, to the summons of death. Two Legs looked out upon the world pretty much as a fox or a hawk looks out upon it: not analytically and self-consciously, but simply with an alert responsiveness to all the animal impulses, from within and without, that constituted the instruction of his life.

Then, as folklore and science agreeingly continue the story of us, there happened to Two Legs the peculiar thing, the thing I was investigating in our earlier chapter, talking of animal personality.

The animal consciousness which he had shared with the other animals was visited by an extraordinary increment. The light of his mind was brightened to where suddenly he could see, in the flash of it, the existence of himself as a self. Henceforth it was open to him not merely to act, but to act in awareness of doing so. Henceforth he was to have not only knowing, but to know that he knew. It had become possible to Two Legs, as to no raccoon or fox, to think the thought: "I am I." Two Legs could now move out of the realm of experiencing into the infinitely stranger and huger realm of realizing.

Whether we say that a soul was breathed into Two Legs, which is the way religious idiom puts it, or simply that the mind of Two Legs took on an enormous enlargement and complication, which is the way a noncommittal naturalist may say it, the fact is there. Two Legs, who had hitherto made his way in the world by the sharpness of his ears and the keenness of his scent and his general maintenance of animal fitness and skill, was now endowed with the unprecedented equipment of self-conscious rationality.

Now Mary and I cannot imagine that any naturalist, unless mystical beyond the edge of madness, would wish to revoke the fateful day when Two Legs's mind took on, so to speak, this new quality of mirror. The humanness given to him and to us, his descendants, is infinitely to be respected.

But it seems important, to naturalists like us, that the light of humanness in his furry skull should not lead to a neglecting or disusing or looking down upon those old, old animal senses that had been his before and that can still be ours.

Of course it is good to think. But it is also good to smell, to hear, and to know by feel. Mary and I like to keep the animal-sense part of us alive.

It isn't likely, to be sure, however long we go animalizing around our patch of earth, that we shall ever be able to see the way a red-tailed hawk can see as it glides in for a landing on a branch of the big dead chestnut over by the southern pasture edge. A hawk has a sense of visual judgment so delicate that it can discriminate lines subtending an angle of twenty-nine seconds. However we train ourselves in "being animals," the deeper to know the lives around us and relish the world, it will scarcely become possible for us to detect temperature changes of a quarter of a degree, as many snakes can. But we find, with practice over the years, that many dulled senses do come into sharpened use. On damp spring evenings in our woods, I have caught the scent of one of the newly hatched big moths before I could see it, clinging to its cocoon with moist wings. Mary opens a window on a winter morning and smells whether snow is coming.

When I felt I was being followed along the road from the mailbox in the June evening, it was only a "feeling," and, as I say, it may have been a perception outside the sensory. But I think not. I think probably without conscious notice I may have heard a little rattle of a pebble or the crackle of a twig. Not impossibly I may have caught, unnoticing, a tiny drift of musk-pungent scent. For Mary and I, by long habit, are alerted to things like this.

At any rate, whatever it was, the feeling persisted and mounted, and presently took over conscious awareness insistently. "Turn around! Turn around!" it said.

It was hardly possible that anything could be following me on this lonely country lane of ours in the fading light. Still. . . . Still. . . .

I whirled around.

Sound, scent, telepathy, whatever, it had not deceived me. I was being followed.

My follower, as I whirled, was not over ten yards from my heels. He had been trotting briskly, and now he came to a hasty squatting stop, sat down on his haunches, and looked at me with his head cocked. My follower was a fox cub.

I stood still as a stump and we peered at each other.

The cub was probably not much more than two months old, for foxes in our neighborhood are most commonly born in March or April. For at least the first month of their lives or longer, little foxes, as a rule, don't even emerge from the den entrance; and after that for several weeks—often until latter summer—a fox youngster stays with his family group and doesn't venture off on solitary excursions. As I stood motionless, watching the cub, I listened for any sound of others of his family, but I could hear nothing.

As casually as I could, I turned around and resumed my homeward walk, but with my head turned to glance back over my shoulder.

The moment I started, the little fox got to his feet and came pattering behind me. He trotted with his head still cocked a little to one side, watching me with intent fascination.

In the next few hundred yards, I stopped perhaps half a dozen times. Each time my foxlet also immediately stopped, sat down, watched me eagerly, and waited. He was a very chubby, fuzzy little fox. (In adulthood our foxes are lean and lithe, but a youngster is much fatter and woollier.) He had big peaked furry ears and puppy-paws, and even when he was sitting still, during my halts to confront him, he kept making little eager wiggles, the way a puppy does when it is urging resumption of some interrupted fun.

When I left the lane and turned in at our gate, the fox cub stood irresolute for a moment or two and then slipped into the underbrush at the side of the road. The last I saw of him, he was crouched among the dusty leaves, his alert little face peeking out intently at my vanishing figure. He craned to watch me until I disappeared into the house, his bright little eyes shining with curiosity, his furry roly-poly body fairly quivering with the intensity of shyly eager friendliness.

When Mary came out with me in a moment to meet this young neighbor of ours, he had vanished. We looked as far up the lane as we could see, and there, just rounding the bend, our fox cub was hurrying away into the darkness, doubtless to rejoin the fox family he had left for his impulsive little excursion in friendship with a naturalist.

Among the countless tales told to illustrate the woods wit of foxes, there is a story that a hunted fox sometimes runs in a great circle and then ingeniously catches up with the hunter from behind and trots along in security in his footsteps, the hunted trailing the hunter. This does happen quite often, as a matter of fact. Perhaps it is a showing of feral cunning. But, remembering an adventure with a pattering little cub on a summer evening, Mary and I sometimes wonder whether these follow-the-hunter episodes may now and then have another explanation. We wonder whether possibly a man-following fox may perhaps occasionally be just curious, just playful, or just making a timid and tentative kind of little gesture of affection.

Foxes are wild and wary. But somewhere, in the depths of that wild heart, there is what also makes a dog.

Way back in the beginning of things, when our ancestor Two Legs had received the light of mind and in the gleam of it was making his first gestures of humanity, the animal whose wary curiosity and shy overtures toward comradeship won his response and thereby began adoption as the first of his dogs, undoubtedly belonged to the family of *Canidae*. No naturalist can guess exactly what animal it was. The beginning of dogs is lost in the ancient mists. The *Canidae* include all the wolves, the jackals, and the foxes. But it is sure that the first dog was a cousin, at least, or a second cousin or a third or a fifth, of the pointed-eared, brush-tailed wild neighbor of Mary's and mine—*Vulpes fulva,* the red fox—that yaps and squalls in our woods, runs pattering and pawing for meadow mice in our snow-drifted fields, and leaves his musky scent hanging in the heavy evening air when he pads along his trail at Fox Crossing to drink at our brook. No one whistled to *Vulpes fulva* back in the morning of the world. He has remained an altogether wild dog, like the wolves. But when you know him as close as a neighbor, as Mary and I do, you are forever finding his doglike qualities, untamed, unwon from original wild allegiances, but there.

One bitter winter morning a few years ago I was up in the heart of our hemlock woods. It was one of those mornings so cold that the world seems frozen, as if forever, in arrest and stillness: the hemlocks bowed under snow, the earth vanished under mounds of snow, a silent whiteness locking everything. I was standing motionless, getting my breath after the long slogging walk through the drifted woods. Not even a chickadee stirred to sound its brisk little winter-defying music or send a small shower of scattered flakes down from the evergreen tops. There was no motion in the icy air. I moved aside a snow-laden hemlock bough and toiled forward deeper into the ghostly stillness of the cold woods.

Perhaps thirty feet ahead of me there burst, silently, an explosion in the snow.

Up came the peaked ears and pointed muzzle of a fox.

With a jump and a shake and a shower of snowflakes, he sprang up from the snow hollow where, undoubtedly, he had been sleeping. Except in their mating time, our foxes sleep without shelter. In the snow a fox beds down by turning around and around, dog-fashion, until he has made a sheltering hollow in a drift, and then he curls up with his brushy tail wrapped around over his nose and dark-stockinged forepaws.

The fox stood looking at me alertly, but he made no move to run away. This was very odd. Foxes are the wariest of our animal neighbors, and any animal startled from sleep assumes danger. Probably, I thought, the fox had not yet "placed" me as a human being, for from the first instant of his tumultuous breakout from his sleeping place I had stood perfectly motionless, just another snow-flecked silent object in a world of white silence.

But then, as fox and I regarded each other steadily, it seemed to me that he was staring so fixedly and sniffing the icy air so carefully from such a very little distance away, that he could not possibly be missing the truth about me. It was as though there were a kind of spell between us.

When some minutes had passed—really only some seconds, I suppose—I broke the spell. I reached out and snapped off a stick of dead hemlock. It made a *crack!* like gunshot in the frosty stillness. Considerably hampered by my heavy jacket, I drew back my arm and shied the hemlock stick at the fox.

The stick dropped into the fluffy snow several feet short of him.

It seemed to me it had scarcely landed when the fox plunged forward toward me in great springing leaps, pounced on the stick, grabbed it, and whirled away. With the ducking, weaving prance of a triumphant collie, he bounded off through the snow, his treasure gripped in his narrow jaws. He ran as hard as he could go now, trotting, jumping, floundering, and struggling through the white depths. In a moment or two he had vanished among far snow-bowed evergreens. I was alone in the winter silence.

However much a naturalist loves his animal neighbors, he dislikes false sentimentality about them. But I don't believe I have to be ashamed to say that as I stood, still motionless with astonishment in the bitter woods, I felt a certain pricking in my eyes not altogether from the cold. No one, as I said a while ago, seems to have whistled to *Vulpes fulva* back in the dawn of things. No one threw him a stick. But there is a part of him—just shown me on a winter morning, as a secret might be trusted to a friend—that for all the millenniums of lonely wildness has perhaps been ready and waiting.

The place called Fox Crossing, in Mary's and my private geography of the small world we possess, is so known to us because it is the place where we most often see foxes cross our little dirt road on their way to the brook to drink or to the low-lying pasture flat to hunt meadow mice and woodchucks. It is a much dimmer and narrower trail than at a deer crossing;

but if we start from the side of the lane and work upland, it is possible by going carefully to follow it all the way up the hillside, across the overgrown fields, through the sumac scrub and the thickets of partridgeberry and hawthorn. Making our way slowly and watchfully along this hill trail, we find other evidences that our foxes are little wild dogs. We find their caches.

All dogs like to take their leftover bones and oddments of food surplus and either bury them or tuck them away in hiding places for future recovery. The ten-pound little wild dog with the red-yellow back, black-stockinged legs and white-tipped brushy tail is no exception.

In Mary's and my experience with our fox neighbors, *Vulpes* seldom actually buries his treasures and tidbits in the earth; but he strews them along his trails according to his own methods of caching. As we go slowly up the hillside from Fox Crossing, we keep our eyes open for odd-looking little heaps of dead leaves or bunches of withered grass at the path's edge. I move one of these aside with the tip of my stick, and there, tucked neatly in shallow hiding, are the bony remains of a woodchuck, or the furry little head with ears still intact of a small cottontail. Sometimes the fox has scratched and scraped a little shower of earth over the cache for further concealment.

Quite often, along this fox path and other ones, Mary and I have found the velvety little bodies of moles. These are seldom covered at all and seem just to have been casually dropped. I don't think we have ever found one that had the slightest tear or tooth mark. Foxes have a trait familiar to every countryman who owns a dog. They are irresistibly tempted to catch moles; but they hate the taste of them.

Foxes, of course, are by formal definition Carnivora. They are eaters of meat. But when you come to know them intimately around the years, you make the discovery that this labeling is misleading. Except formally, foxes are less carnivores than omnivores. When a fox works his way slowly and intently across a field, crisscross, crisscross, he pounces and snaps a great many more times than if he were hunting only mice, chucks, and the like. With binoculars Mary and I have watched scores of foxes' hunting expeditions across our fields and we have been able to see something of the variety of their catches. Probing dried fox droppings, brought home for examination under our low-powered microscope, I have learned a good deal more. Foxes are catchers of beetles, crickets, and grasshoppers. They eat caterpillars and chrysalids. Frequently on early-morning hunts through the drenched pasture, a fox catches earthworms. Perhaps most unexpectedly, but very often, a fox eats tufts of tender young grass.

Aesop's fox, in the fable, was fond of grapes. That part is not a fable. The grapes in our woods-edge garden (very sour grapes they are, as it happens) have often been nipped off the gnarled old vines by our fox neighbors in the autumn. One of the late fall happenings that Mary and I most look forward to seeing each year, toward the latter part of November when our first heavy snows come sifting down over the withered countryside, is the first nocturnal visit of a fox to our orchard.

We look out from the little bedroom windows of our old farmhouse into the cold moonlight shining on the ancient apple trees, snow-dusted now, under which, in hot weather, old Dan and Frolic so often stand. Has our fox come yet? Sometimes several nights go by. And then one night, staring out, we see him: a stealthy little dog, slipping through the moonlight, continually darting glances to right, left, and over his shoulder. He stands still, listening. He patters forward again through the fresh snow, leaving his unmistakable little single-line dog trail, and then perhaps he stands again motionless and alert, this time with one forepaw drawn up and his lean muzzle thrust sharply forward. It is a characteristic fox pose, as much so as the one in which he likes to "sit tall" on a high lookout point on our summer hillside, with his four paws bunched compactly together and his chin tilted up. He points, pauses, listens again in the cold moonlight. Then Mary and I see him slip into the dark shadow under one of the old trees, and in a moment he begins pawing and scratching away the snow. He has found something now. He stands munching and crunching. He is feasting on frozen apples.

We have never seen a fox touch the fallen apples of late summer and early autumn. But the moment the really cold weather comes, and the first snow, our fox remembers them. When there has been a good apple year (or as good as our old trees ever have; we keep them as shade for the horses and as living quarters for woodpeckers and bluebirds and White-foot, the deer mouse, and don't try to attend to them as orchardists would) he subsists on them as a food staple all winter. It is astonishing how many of the half-rotted little fruits, frozen stone-hard, his fox stomach can hold. Sometimes Mary and I stand watching him from the window for as long as an hour, while he scarcely pauses in his absorbed digging and munching.

A fat grouse sleeping on a low evergreen branch in the woods; a cottontail not quite quick enough at zigzagging and circling from brush pile to brier patch; a nest of baby meadow larks in the tall field grass; a cluster of wild blackberries or huckleberries; a green-skinned frog pounced upon among the reeds at the edge of a brook pool—any of these things or any of a hundred others provide food for our musky little fox with the brushy tail and the sharp-pointed nose. Once, just after Mary and I had seen a fox go pattering across the lane at Fox Crossing, we found on his trail, still warm, the remains of a mourning dove. He must have caught that, I imagine, by stalking it on the ground when it was feeding. A fox can ground-stalk as patiently and stealthily as a cat. He creeps forward with infinite slowness, belly against the earth, eyes shining, lean muzzle thrust far forward and almost touching the ground. Another time, when we saw a fox make a catch over by the tumble-down stone wall along the south pasture border, we were puzzled by the fact that he kept shaking his head, jumping, throwing up his head, and shaking it again. Only after some minutes were we able to figure that out. He had caught a snake. Dogwise, he was whipping and snapping it.

From autumn until past the turn of the year, the male foxes of our countryside go solitary. The fox keeps entirely to himself, pattering around our frozen woods and fields in search of what parts of his widely miscellaneous diet are available. I see him in the thin gray light of the early winter mornings, working his way slowly up the eastern meadow slope, sniffing, watching, pawing, to find meadow mice in their snow tunnels. He makes the ascent of the field in a great wide zigzag, covering almost every foot of it. I watch him until his lonely little figure, still just identifiable by the big brush and the pointed ears, disappears at last over the white edge of the ridge. Then Mary and I meet him again, or a brother of his, when we go for our winter-evening walk along the snow-banked lane. He is trotting fast now, with his head down, still hunting in the icy dusk. We always "freeze," of course, the instant we see him; and I am always hoping that miraculously there may be another chance for me to make a fox for an instant my dog, by shying a stick for him to carry, or there may be another experience of having a fox come trotting at my heels. But our lean-muzzled neighbor halts for just a second, stiffening, watching us with narrowed eyes, and then wheels away and bolts off through the wintry darkness.

In the middle of the winter nights, Mary and I listen to the yapping barking of our foxes. It is one of the most familiar sounds of home to us, in the still, cold, ice-sheathed season of our western Berkshire countryside. In severe winters, our dirt road is often snow-blocked for days at a time. The hundred-odd acres of our naturalist's world, always sequestered, become a world isolated entirely. We are alone with our animal neighbors for fair. In the intense stillness and cold of the night, we listen to the creak and cracking of the bare bones of the trees; we cock our heads and listen to catch the first faint far hum of the snowplow turning off the county road to come laboring our way through the gale-blown drifts that stretch from fence to fence; we listen to the foxes bark.

Sometimes two foxes call back and forth to each other, like wolves across northern tundra. *Yap! Yap! Yoooo!* The bark rings out from far up on the hill. We can picture the small wild dog making it, sitting on a snowy escarpment up toward Owl Rock, looking out over the glimmering valley. His head is tilted up toward the stars, and his fox breath makes a cloud in the still cold air. *Yap! Yap! Yap-yap!* Very faint and far away, toward the southeast, comes a bark of answering. That must be a fox over at the edge of the steep dark woods beyond the Pileated Tree. Mary and I open a window wider, and bundle ourselves up, and stand looking out into the wintriness, listening. Back and forth the calls go, now fainter, now louder, now their directions changing as the two foxes go trotting off on their respective trails through the night. Presently they die away altogether, and there is only the silence and cold.

By February, we are aware of a change in the night

voices. This change is one of our earliest signs of spring.

Spring, of course, comes on the twenty-first of March, if you go by the calendar. But calendar-reckoning is an arbitrary affair, composed for purposes of neat accountancy. Naturalists like Mary and me go by our earth calendar which is different.

As I mentioned when I was talking about our woodchucks, Mary and I have gone out every ground-hog day, the second of February, for many years, and rarely have failed to find that at least one of our woodchuck neighbors has come scrabbling up from under the frost line. The woodchuck says it is spring, and we agree with that. What else is it but spring when the life juices start running again, and sleep is broken, and eyes look out once more on the glory of the world? So a woodchuck says to us; and there is much else in our woods and fields to say it to us, even in February, even many weeks before the calendar-marked solstice in March. Snow may continue to come down, but in the willows along our brook there is a suffusion of pinks and greens. Our moles start coming out. We find where they have gone floundering over land (or over snow), which is not a wintry thing to do but a spring thing. In the first week of February we cut pussy-willow sprays and we find them all sapful and full of eagerness. While it is still February, we come upon a cawing and anticking and uproar of crows, up along the wood road among the hemlocks; and it is unquestionably spring; for this is courting. Nor is it bird-courting time only for the crows, raising their delighted hubbub of love and competition in the evergreen woods. One of these cold, bright February days, we hear a hearty chirruping from the direction of the door of our old barn. I go over there (needing my boots, perhaps, to flounder through snowdrifts, but it is irrelevant) and I see a scraggle of straw showing under the old door cap. The English sparrows are nesting. It is possible, of course, that the thermometer will again slide down toward zero. But there is nothing wintry in this cold, bright day for Mary and me. Our sparrows are in their springtime.

In the February nights, as perhaps our most eloquent signal of all the presolstice stir of beginnings, there is the sound of our foxes in their springtime.

We still hear the sharp barks and yappings that the little dog foxes have made all winter. But now there is a new sound mixing in with it. It is a hoarse, shrill squalling, a kind of yell. There is an immeasurable wildness in it. It rises in a wailing, over in the black woods beyond the pasture; it dies away in throaty snarls somewhere up on the hill. The female foxes, the vixens, are crying. It is our wild dogs' breeding time.

Some fifty-one days from now, in the darkness of their den burrow or "earth," a new generation of narrow-eyed, perkeared, wary little fox neighbors of ours will be being born. The promise of it is not only in the squallings and snarlings we hear in the night, but also in the rank gusts of fox scent we catch as we go out to make our animalizing rounds of our snowy acres in the morning. Foxes are always foxy-smelling, with such an acrid mustiness that even the young cub who trotted after me along the lane may have first let me know of his presence, as I suggested, by a little drift of scent which I took into my nostrils without taking it into my conscious mind. But in the tumult of their breeding season in late winter (or, as Mary and I should say, the spring) male foxes become particularly pungent, and they are continually voiding jets of their musky urine against snow banks and the boles of trees. In the heavy air of thawing February mornings, the wild-dog scent is as familiar an odor of our countryside as is a few weeks later the rank vegetable pungence of the skunk cabbages thrusting up their fleshy green spathes from the wet black loam beside the brook.

A den which has probably supplied many of the foxes of our neighborhood is far up on the hill, in a plateau field of stubble and coarse grass that once upon a time, many years ago, was an alfalfa lot. It is unlikely that foxes originally dug the burrow, for the soil is clayey and rocky. A fox is an effective digger in soft sandy earth, but in any other terrain usually just adapts and enlarges an already existent cavity. This fox den was almost certainly originally a woodchuck burrow.

It has been a fox den, however, ever since Mary and I discovered it a number of years ago; and every summer, on our occasional visits to sit at the edge of the field and watch it, we see it have more and more a fox-den look. By this I mean that the burrow mouth, once just large enough to let *Marmota monax* come waddling out of it to sit up tent-peg-straight and gaze around the field and chirrup his woodchuck whistles, every year has grown wider and wider, until in recent seasons it has become probably a foot and a half across. (A very little way inside, the tunnel narrows, but its vestibule keeps being pawed out, apparently by successive fox generations.) Also, from all around the burrow, there radiate more and more clearly beaten fox trails. One of them goes on over across the hill and vanishes in heavy woods beyond the limit of our acres. Another leads to the old stone wall at the edge of the field and there it vanishes. I make the guess that from that point foxes must patter along the top of the wall. Still another trail winds away diagonally down the scrub-grown hillside fields to the northwest, and eventually becomes the trail leading to the place that Mary and I call Fox Crossing.

Fox families using this den have renovated the whole original woodchuck labyrinth. The two onetime "bolt holes," twenty-five or thirty feet from the den's main doorway, have been greatly enlarged from their woodchuck size, though retaining their almost perfectly circular shape. For all the subterranean digging foxes must have done, enlarging and adapting underground passageways and storage rooms, we have never discovered any signs of freshly excavated earth. The foxes scatter it scrupulously, or ram and tamp it into side chambers of the original woodchuck construction, in an exercise of the same shy guile they show in so many other aspects of their wary lives. It is natural to a fox to keep breaking and confusing his trail even when there is no pursuit: to bound back and forth over an old stone wall, to spring in big jumps from boulder to boulder across our brook, to go pattering along a fence rail and then drop down for a while and then jump up on the rail again. It is natural to a fox to try to keep his den a secret. But there is no concealing the tracks that paws have worn to the site in the old alfalfa field, or the telltale bits of bones, feathers, and rabbitskins that accumulate around the den door as spring passes into summer, or the giveaway fox smell that clings to the place. Even in winter, when the den is in disuse, I have knelt in the snow and poked my head into the cold burrow mouth and have smelled the lingering mustiness of the foxes of the season before.

Mary and I make our way to the old alfalfa field perhaps half a dozen times a summer. We always mean to go oftener; but it is a long hike there on a hot night, and we have learned from experience that even when we are positive there is a fox family in residence, these timid and alert neighbors of ours can be extraordinarily hard to see. Perhaps as we approach their field, going as cautiously as we can among the pines that have sprung up in hundreds in the thin rocky soil of the hilltop, we miscalculate the wind a little, or it shifts suddenly. Or we snap a twig inadvertently, or we dislodge a stone from one of the old fences as we climb over, or whatever. Then we can wait until dark and see no foxes. The big triangular ears listen with a special acuteness in family time. The continually lifted noses of mother and father fox—the vixen at the den entrance with her youngsters, the dog fox very likely sitting on a high lookout point—are after all dog noses, and dog noses at their wild subtlest.*

Besides these discouragements, there is the fact that naturalists like Mary and me, when we set out for a far part of our neighborhood, are forever being sidetracked or stopped by some animal adventure long before we get there. Meaning to make our way, on speculation, to the distant fox field, we start off up the wood road or follow the narrow faint trail across the overgrown upland fields from Fox Crossing, and in the first five minutes we meet a woodchuck, or we meet a deer, or we meet a coon or a cottontail, or likely as not we meet a here-at-hand fox; and there goes the expedition. Any opportunity to enter into deeper and more intimate knowing of any animal neighbor of ours is too attractive to be forgone. We can get lost for an hour or two or three not only in something so rare as a coon household close-up or a chance to hear the soft secret murmur of a baby screech owl, but just in watching White-foot peek out of an apple-tree hollow, just in studying the print of coon paws in the mud of the brook bank, just in thinking about a thing like this and then letting thought wander off in woods-wonderings and earth-thinkings

* What the most sensorily-aware naturalist's ears, straining, can hear at the farthest a hundred and seventy-five yards away is audible to dog ears a distance of over a mile. Dr. F. J. J. Buytendijk of the University of Groningen, testing dogs' sense of smell, found canine nostrils able to detect iodoform in a solution of one part to four million.

and rambling speculation. I don't suppose we have been able to watch fox youngsters at the den in the distant hilltop field more than five or six times altogether. But those few successful watchings have been a great reward.

The setting sun shines very late on the fox-den field. Long after evening has come to our lowlands, even when the dusk has so deepened toward darkness that hawk moths have come to the garden and the last chiming evening songs of wood thrushes have died away in the shadowy trees, the field on the hilltop plateau is still red-golden in the light of the sun slipping behind the Catskills. It is in this coppery suffusion of sunset that we see our fox cubs. As they play together, or just sit on their broad little puppylike haunches and stare around the world they have not yet gone exploring, they glow warmly golden, almost orange.

Foxes may have from four to nine young ones in a litter; but we have not seen more than four at any time. As I was saying earlier, they look more like little dogs now than they do when they have grown up. The vixen, lying in the entrance of the den with just her head, forepaws, and shoulders showing, is lean, narrow-muzzled, all spare and compact; but her cubs are fuzzily woolly, splay-pawed, and bumbly, in the way of puppies. Mary and I watch as they roughhouse together, tumbling, biting, jumping, and prancing stiff-legged in feints and teases, and it is difficult to think that these are wild animals, presently to become crafty and as furtive as shadows as they patter through the night. The country place of Mary's girlhood was called Foxfield. In our own fox field, its coarse brown grass all aflame with sunset, its family of little wild dogs unrealizing that any eye watches them, we take the foxness of our fox-neighbors close to us, so to speak, in such an intimacy as Mary was accustomed to dream about.

Only once have we seen a fox cub make any gesture toward going more than a few feet away from the entrance of the den. Mostly the cubs caper and tussle very close under their mother's watch. What happened on this occasion was a curious thing to see.

The little cub apparently heard or saw something far off at the western edge of the field, and abruptly, with an oddly adult-fox look—muzzle thrust forward, eyes alertly intent on whatever it was—went trotting straight off through the golden light. We saw the vixen stir a little, uneasily, and then in a moment or two slip out of the den entrance and stand up. We thought she was going to dart after her wanderer, run around him, and head him back. She did not.

She just "pointed" with her sharp muzzle in the direction of his retreating little form and stood rigidly silent and still. She did not make a sound, or at least none that our human ears could hear. But in a few seconds the little cub began to waver in his steps, and then, uncertainly, he slowed down and stopped. He turned quickly around and looked straight at his mother. She kept her level gaze on him. As if pulled by an invisible thread, the little fox came hurrying for home.

Our fox-field family stays a unit until into the autumn; but as time passes the vixen relaxes her watchful control, and the father fox very gradually introduces the cubs into farther and farther excursions from the den by dropping the foods he brings home at an ever-increasing distance. He lays a fat frog or a meadow mouse at the edge of the field and stands over it, coaxing. He trots along the old stone wall, head high, brush waving, with a cottontail dangling in his jaws, and invites his cubs to come and get it. Foxes initiate their young ones into hunting-skill by a long process of education. Once on a hot September evening, when Mary and I had been watching the fox den from behind a pine tree for an hour or more and had about decided we were to have no glimpse of fox life that night, we saw the father fox come stealthily along the stone wall, crouching close to it, with something in his jaws. Suddenly he sat down, head held high, and we could make out that what he was carrying was a rabbit. We could make out, too, that it was alive. He must have caught and carried it with delicate skill. He had sat erect only a second or two when four cubs burst out, not from the den we had been watching so fixedly but from a growth of underbrush in the next field where we had not looked at all. They raced toward their father. When they had nearly reached him, he dropped the rabbit. The cottontail can scarcely have made a zigzag run of more than twenty feet before four rushing, pouncing, little red-furred wild dogs had caught it. They stood huddled over their catch, pawing, snuffing, prancing away and back again in delighted triumph. Plainly, our chubby little puppies of the spring had come to their fulfillment. They were ready to be foxes.

By winter the fox family is permanently broken up. Each little fox has come to go alone, sounding his bark in our snowy woods, warily visiting the orchard to dig for frozen apples under the moon. Except in his own mating time to come, his life from now on is lonely wildness.

Lonely wildness; but always also, deep in the heart of it, there is the dogness. There is the shy hint of approachability. There is the trace, down under all the fox wariness, of a persisting love of puppy fun. It may happen only once that a cub trots at my heels, or a fox takes a shied stick in the winter woods. But in our long knowing of our neighbor *Vulpes fulva* Mary and I have caught again and again glimpses of this fox spirit that made those two adventures possible. I think of a quiet little happening close to home one summer evening a year or two ago.

We had gone to the pasture to take the heifers their evening grain.

This is always a happy time of day for us. Heifers have a fine meadow-animal smell about them; and it is good to stand knee-deep in the grass and tansy, and have them butting and bumping and nuzzling, and listen to their little sighs and whoofs of contentment as they munch their oats, with the last long golden slant of the evening sun across their tawny backs.

But this evening the heifers did not come lolloping to the gate bars in their customary eager fashion. They were standing far away on the distant slope of the pasture hill. They stood all close together, in the formation of a tight herd, with their heads down like watchful bison. Then, suddenly, they began to run.

They ran faster than I have ever seen cattle run before, their heads still down, thrust forward; and as they thundered along they kept formation. Clearly, they were chasing something. With every ounce of their strength, they were in pursuit of some fleeing thing in the tall grass.

In a moment we saw what it was; for it made a great leap above the level of the thistles and mulleins and flung its head back over its shoulder to see its pursuers. It was a fox.

The heifers, we supposed, would drive it out of the pasture; and in a few moments there would be only the quiet evening; and we would have seen something a little odd, but quickly to be forgotten among greater country excitements.

But we have not forgotten. For that is not the way it went.

The way it went was a great sweeping circular chase which brought the fox at last to the western fence—but when he got there he did not run from the pasture. He circled in again; and the whole thundering pursuit, around and around the forty acres, started a new lap.

We understood.

This was not some affair of life and death. This was not even a scene of anger. This was playing. This was a game.

This was six animals, caught up in the tumult of the summer earth and the golden evening, having fun.

We stood at the pasture gate, and watched and watched; and it was so.

I don't know how many rushing rounds the animals had made when the heifers began to tire; but presently, all laboring and breathing hard, they clumped to a halt. With the slowing and stopping of the noise of their hoofbeats, the fox slowed and stopped too. He sat down on his lean haunches beside the small black walnut tree, and cocked an ear and an eye at the resting heifers, and lolled his red tongue and grinned.

Oh, "grinned" is anthropomorphic, of course. But not very. If foxes cannot smile, they can wear a look of a kind of infective frolicking, as dogs can, as of a vast interior smile subsuming them from heads to tails. This fox was like that.

When all the animals were rested, there was resumption of their game. Sometimes it was running. Sometimes it was hardly more than walking. Fun, after all, cannot be conjured. Animals let it rise and dwindle in its own rhythm as it will. The game went on and on, and then on again, now fast, now slow, now pausing altogether; and all the while a red fox absorbed in it, grinning.

We watched until the last light had gone behind our western hills and a whippoorwill was calling from the blackberry patch. We came back slowly to our dark house, extraordinarily happy, to wait for the rising of the moon.

Meeting Mephitis

"Hi! Come here! Quick!"

On a morning in late March I was working at my study desk, and Mary had gone out for a walk. We were having a heavy spring snowstorm. The big wet flakes of "robin snow" were swirling down so densely that I could scarcely see as far as the split-rail fence, and snow was bowing the pines and capping the bud-pink twig tips of the maples.

When Mary was a small prenaturalist in Wicklow, she used to exult in the roaring storms that swept in from the sea over the Irish cliffs; and she has been exulting in storms ever

233

since, the more deeply as her nature insight has grown, and the more enthusiastically the fiercer the storm. On almost any day of savage weather, I can be pretty sure to hear a door close and see the bundled-up figure of Mary slipping out into the midst of the blow. A naturalist thinks about the weather in a particular nature-minded way in terms of that Wholeness we were saying something about in connection with our cottontail neighbors; and Mary has this sense of broad interrelations and over-all earth pattern, weatherwise, particularly.

A snowstorm, it is true, may hold up our mail. But, considered in a wider sense, it is this same snow that quilts and saves the vegetation, and leaches slowly into the earth and waters it, and that thus is strictly responsible for the green glory of next summer. It would be stretching things only a little, in one of those dramatic exaggerations that Thoreau loved, to say that it is only because there is snow that there is any mail to be delayed in reaching us. For the role of snow in preserving Northern vegetations is very nearly vital; and without vegetations there would not only be no letters, there would be none of us at all.

It is easy to grow fretful about "too much rain." But the surface of the land is only a little portion of what requires to be watered. To be nature-minded is to extend your mind's vision to the deep water tables under the ground, and to be aware of how vitally the natural economy is dependent on their maintenance. In many places in our country, the water table has fallen to twice as far below the surface as it originally

234

was. In one Middle Western state it has fallen from eight feet underground to fifty-nine feet underground. Today, the most prolonged rainy spells of "bad weather" are hardly enough to sustain the level of the waters under the earth on which we depend for all our wells and springs and the health of deep roots. To see the whole picture, nature-mindedly, is to realize not only the importance of bad weather but the interlinked importance of certain "bad" features of the natural landscape: swamps, marshes, bogs, natural ponds, and little shallow lakes.

Swamps function, in the economy of the whole, to collect rains and melted snows and to feed the water very, very slowly into the earth so that it gradually makes its way to the subterranean water table. Forests, where the dead trees and the fallen leaves decay to make a spongy matted floor, function to the same end. It was failure to see this wholeness of things, and draining sloughs and clearing away forests, that created these disastrous conditions of quick run-off, erosion, and falling water tables that so much conservation effort is now needed to remedy. If you keep your vision narrow, a day of pouring rain in a swampy landscape may look a sullen and dreary thing. But the farther you see into the creation's wholeness, the closer you come to rejoicing in rain as delightedly as in sunshine and to rejoicing in swamps as delightedly as in any golden upland.

The furious thunderstorms of midsummer perhaps tempt to a shortsighted irritation with the nature of things. Surely, this tempestuous uproar that snaps branches and smashes trees, that beats and buffets small birds to death with its fury —surely the most infatuatedly sentimental naturalist can scarcely rejoice in that? But in fact the sentimentality does not lie with a naturalist. There is no sentimentality in the vision of the Whole. On the contrary, there is a rigorousness. What culls the weak trees in a forest? What agency lops away deadwood, plucks out the weakest or stupidest individuals from a species of bird or animal, and as it were, flogs the lazing or dulling biota into new alertness and fresh health? What but such tempests? It is naturalists, as Mary would say, looking large-mindedly upon the creation, who pronounce it good. It is sentimentalists who refuse acknowledgment that what is good may also be terrible and stern; or that the death of the particular may have its place in the healthiness of the whole.

So she had gone out this morning to enjoy the bad weather.

Having had a look at a kingfisher rattling along our brook and perching, impossibly blue, among the snowy willow branches overhanging it, and having toured the pasture to see how our woodchuck neighbors were taking the snow swirl that sifted into their freshly dug burrows on this spring morning, she had circled back toward the house through the pelting whiteness, and it was obvious that now, close to home, she had run into a major animal adventure.

"Hi! Hi! Hurry!"

I threw on my jacket and hat and ran out into the storm to join her.

She was over by the big elm which has played a considerable part in our closest-to-home experiences with wild neighbors. One of our climbing woodchucks once ascended almost to the top of it and gave us the chance to see exactly what technique this tubby marmot uses on his excursions aloft. It is this big elm that is specially thronged with warblers in spring-migration time, and it is on the outermost high twig tips of this tree that every year our Baltimore orioles attach their pensile nests of woven fibers. Mary's animal adventure now, however, was not occurring *up* in the tree. She was staring down at the snowy earth at the base of it. As I ran toward her, she motioned me to slow down and come cautiously. I noticed for the first time that Mary was not standing altogether still, in the customary "freeze" of meeting an animal neighbor. Oddly enough, I could see now, amid the almost blinding snowflakes, she was very slowly, very warily, walking backward.

A moment later I was close enough to know why.

The animal she had met at the base of the elm was our neighbor *Mephitis* the skunk. And this skunk was in extraordinary trouble. Wedged tightly over his head, pressing almost against his shoulders, was a tin can.

At the waddly, rocking gait of skunks, which is like the gait of our coons but more so, the skunk was pattering distractedly around the base of the big elm. He turned now this way, now that way, making a little rush in one direction, reversing himself, circling, now standing still and swinging his imprisoned head furiously. Every time Mary made a backward step of retreat, as cautiously and softly as she stepped in the fresh snow, the skunk detected the motion and at once turned and came blindly in her direction.

It was not surprising that the hurry-up "Hi!" which had fetched me had been of a rather special urgency.

No animal neighbor of all the ones with which Mary and I share our hundred-and-some-acre world is more innocent and more amiable than a skunk. The spirit of this four- or five-pound little black-and-white-striped animal with the bushy, plumy tail is so placid and equable that a skunk strolling through our woods on a summer evening will scarcely jump or hesitate even if he meets a fox head-on on the trail or if suddenly he encounters a naturalist towering over him. The skunk just swerves a little, as in an automatic animal courtesy, or sometimes stands still and waits for the other party to make the detour, and then continues serenely puttering along with his small skunk thoughts given undistractedly to turning over stones and poking into grass tussocks in search of grasshoppers and beetles. Skunks go about rapt in the quiet, happy fulfillments of being skunks: prowling around in their waddling, poking, unhurriedly inquisitive way through the night, meandering along the brook and flipping out a sleeping minnow, waddling in a random way through the pasture to find mice and crickets, strolling over to the moonlit blackberry patch to stuff themselves on the small wild fruits. A skunk follows the most erratic and whimful routes of any animal neighbor of ours. He just meanders, unhurried, unplanning, uncontentious, and serene. Almost nothing bothers him, or ever brings him up sharp and alert, or rouses him out of his mild, contented preoccupations. Someone has described a cat as "a sovereign state with a tail." It makes an excellent description of our neighbor *Mephitis mephitis,* the plumy-tailed little putterer who goes quiet, reserved, and contented, under our moon, in the enormous security of his skunkness.

Mild and amiable as a skunk is, devoted to going his quiet woods way in tranquillity, the fact remains that under molestation or indignity our neighbor *Mephitis* can bring into use a terrible weapon.

Beware, an old axiom puts it, the anger of a patient man. Beware, as a naturalist's version may put it, the anger of a patient skunk. Let *Mephitis* just go his meandering way through the twilight, scratching for June-bug grubs, hunting for a drowsy colony of bees, idling and poking along through our woods and fields, and he is as gentlehearted a little wayfarer as ever went peaceably upon his animal rounds. But threaten him, hurt him, make enough assault on the sovereign state of his skunk personality, and he can be provoked to what is nearly literally an explosion. He can be provoked to firing his tail gun.

This weapon of *Mephitis,* wherewith to defend his right to pursue unmolested his pattering little nocturnal excursions, consists of two anal glands under the root of his waving brushy tail. Normally they are hidden in his thick posterior fur. They hold an ammoniacal, burning, acrid sulfide of such pungence that a jet of it, voided on a humid summer night over by the Pileated Tree at the far southern edge of our acres, has been easily detectable by Mary and me as far away as our Owl Rock on the top of the northern hill. The stench *Mephitis* can loose is terrible not in its flavor but in its intensity. Magnify any sensation enough and it becomes a distress. Light is agreeable to eyes; but brighten it sufficiently and it becomes blinding. Sound is welcome to ears; but increase its volume beyond a point and it becomes unendurable. This is the way it is with skunk stench. Drifting over our darkened countryside, the thin, diluted hint of it coming in to us through our opened windows in the night is an odor of animalness, wildness, earthness that is as enjoyable, to naturalists like us, as the smell of brook water, woods loam, fox musk, or the house of a wintering cottontail in our brush pile. But when a skunk discharges it at close range, it is a concentrate so intense as to be suffocating and blinding. A spatter of drops on your skin burns like acid. A jet of *Mephitis's* fluid in your eyes is an excruciation. Whatever is touched by a skunk's spray is soaked in an odor nearly ineradicable. There is an outcropping of rock in our pasture where one summer evening several years ago a strolling skunk was pounced upon by a great horned owl. For two full years after that, whenever the air was damp and still, I could go to that rock ledge and catch the unmistakable skunk smell still clinging in the interstices of the stones.

Aroused to the unavoidable necessity of defending his quiet skunkness, our neighbor *Mephitis* can hurl a jet of his overpowering scent five or six feet or more with considerable accuracy, and a fine mist or cloud of lesser concentration drifts even farther. A skunk's scent glands are protrusible. *Mephitis* can aim in nearly any direction. If sufficiently harassed, he can perform as many as five or six convulsive squeezes in succession, each time ejecting his paralyzing spume of stench. His sulfide comes out under such pressure that each explosion of a jetting stream discharges only about a twentieth of a teaspoonful from his reservoir.

So here were the three of us, Mary and I and our skunk, under the big elm tree in the pelting March snow, with a problem.

The tin can, after all, was probably our fault. When I tote the garbage up the hill to the hidden pit in the woods, I try to be careful about glass or tin cans or anything else that might harm any of our animal neighbors who make this pit a nightly meeting place. But I am probably forgetful sometimes, being distracted by an animal adventure along the way—or just the singing of an indigo bunting in the sunny brier tangle at the woods edge, just the smell of the wild strawberries on the sidehill, even just the way the cumulus clouds look sailing up over the daisied field on the hilltop, for it is things like this, to be sure, that make neighborhood naturalists the naturalists they are—and it was altogether likely I was responsible for the tin can that had trapped our neighbor. *Mephitis* has been a good neighbor to Mary and me, and much cherished. In his grave, equable little way, he has let us into his life over the years; and we have known him well and loved him. Now here he was in great and peculiar trouble, probably all of my doing.

I considered a minute. Then I motioned Mary away to a safe distance. I dropped to my knees in the snow, narrowed my eyes in an instinctive gesture of protection, and chirruped to our little black-and-white prisoner.

Instantly he turned, lifted his tin-hooded head, and came to me. The tin can bumped against my knees. The skunk backed a few inches and stood still.

Now or never.

I put my hand on his snow-wet back and stroked him.

Under the coarse heavy fur, his body felt extraordinarily small and bony, like a kitten's. He stood perfectly still, except for his forepaws. He kept raising them a little in alternation, as a man under stress may keep shifting his weight from one foot to the other. I stroked some more and mumbled and squeak-talked some more, and the small forepaws stood still. I watched the plumy tail, now draggled with snow. It stayed down in a skunklike signal of trustfulness and unalarm.

With my right hand firmly on the skunk's shoulders, I took hold of the rusted tin can with my left hand and gave a long steady pull.

I could feel the small body stiffen and see the skunk brace his paws, and he seemed to cooperate by pulling backward. But the can did not come off. The top of it had not been entirely removed when it was opened, and when the can was empty the top had been pushed inward. It had been easy for a hungry and inquisitive *Mephitis* to poke his head inside, but the angle of the can lid held him prisoner, almost like a trap treadle, when he tried to withdraw.

I turned the can slowly, worked it forward and backward, turned it some more, pulled, pushed, maneuvered.

As I worked with increasing urgency, the small body of *Mephitis* was all but lifted off the ground with the tugging and twisting. But the snow-draggled tail stayed down, and there was not the sound of a whimper. A skunk is never a very talkative animal. *Mephitis* usually maintains an entire silence as he goes about his grave little skunk wanderings through our country night. But he is not voiceless. He can growl; he can make a coony sort of small churring and muttering; and sometimes he grates his teeth in a chattering like the noise our woodchucks make when something has disturbed them down in their burrows. But there was not a sound now. There was just a squirming, struggling little black-and-white body, cold and snow-wet, making mighty efforts of cooperation.

Suddenly something "gave"—a considerable tuft of fur, as it proved, from our skunk's well-ruffed neck. I rocked back on my heels with a tin can held aloft in my left hand and, under my right hand, a freed skunk blinking his berry-bright little eyes in the sudden snow light.

Someone took the can from my left hand. Mary, who may

sometimes say, for her reasons, that she is not really a naturalist, but who always turns out somehow to think an animal adventure outweighs almost any other consideration, had entirely disregarded my waving her away to a safe distance and had been standing all the while right beside me.

I got to my feet very slowly, so as not to startle our newly freed *Mephitis* by abruptly towering over him, and Mary and I stood quietly together in the storm, white as a pair of snowmen. The skunk sniffed at our feet, peered up at our faces, and then for several magical moments brushed his body and tail back and forth across our legs as a happy cat will do. He gave himself the luxury of a prodigious shaking, spattering us with snow and water. He sniffed a time or two at the snow-filled air, turned from us, and went rocking off in his crooked-tracked way in the direction of where the wood road starts. We stayed still, watching, until his small figure, earnest and preoccupied, had gone floundering out of sight up the trail.

Naturalists who live intimately with animals as Mary and I do, and whose life of animal knowing is at least as much a thing of love as of science, like to be none the less exact about not ascribing to animal personality more than it in fact contains. We want to take animals to us in their honest animality as precisely as a scrupulous naturalist can interpret that. But when analysis is all neatly done, and the limits drawn where you think they belong, well—then here is a small skunk, with a hand grabbing his back as tight as owl talons might grab it, and another hand wrenching and yanking at his imprisoned head and tearing out his fur by the tuft, and it appears he understands the improbable truth that there is affection in this. What in him responds, and to what? What is the stuff of this knowing? I don't answer; I just leave it hanging as Mary and I left it hanging in a long silence between us, as we looked at each other and at the vanishing figure of our small neighbor *Mephitis* puttering off contentedly up the woods trail in the snow.

Skunks don't hibernate, technically speaking. They never fall into the deep life suspension, with all its physiological changes, that our wintering woodchucks undergo. But they winter-drowse as coons do; and most years from about the first of December to the latter part of February or early March, Mary and I seldom meet *Mephitis*. As our first heavy November snows come sifting down—the snows that bring a fox to the orchard, and set cottontails to burrowing deeper into the brush pile, and urge White-foot to a busy roofing and capping of birds' nests—a skunk seeks out a winter den and furnishes it against the bitter weather ahead.

Sometimes a skunk may dig out his own den, scraping away with heavy foreclaws to make a burrow under a big tree root or in a rock crevice; but as a rule he makes use of an already existent burrow, only enlarging and adapting it a little, often not altering it at all. The skunks of our neighborhood, in nine cases out of ten, retire into woodchuck burrows to spend the two or three months of severest weather in company with the oblivious woodchuck tenant who has slipped into his profound unconsciousness weeks before. A skunk likes particularly a chuck burrow close to the woods edge, or one of those dug in the shelter of a big rock or underneath one of our old stone walls. When *Mephitis* has solemnly inspected the burrow and found plenty of room in it, he makes trip after trip, in his earnest leisurely way, lugging hay, tufts of withered pasture grass and dead leaves, until his selected area of the burrow has been proofed against the coldest weather. Then he withdraws into this security and composes himself for a drowsing wait for spring.

Sometimes he is alone; more often he finds himself part of a considerable skunk company. Upwards of half a dozen skunks may troop into the same burrow to share communal warmth. In skunks' family time, the group in a den is just the mother skunk and her babies. Father skunk, as a rule, stays away. But in the winter den-up, skunks may nestle together in an amiable miscellany—a male, two or three females, and some maturing youngsters of either sex from the previous spring's litters. Dozing companionably together, one or another of the company now and then rousing on a mild day and pattering out for a few hundred yards' excursion, the band of skunks sleeps and idles away the worst of the winter.

There is an old woodchuck burrow on a steep stony hillside not far from the Muskrat Pool which has for years been a popular wintering place for our skunk neighbors. It is dug under the roots of a twisted witch-hazel. As far as Mary and I have been able to discover, no woodchuck has lived in it for a long while. It is entirely surrendered to wintering skunks. On mild midwinter days when we go out to see the stir of life that even a very brief spell of such weather may bring to our neighborhood—the flight, for instance, of a mourning-cloak butterfly trying its wings in the pale winter sunshine in our snowy woods—we often go over to this den, and we see a maze of skunk prints all around the mouth of it. On such a day we don't go very close. To go close, we wait for a bitterly cold day when the snow is blue-white and squeaks under our boots and we can feel certain that *Mephitis* is numbed to a deep drowsiness. Then we kneel in the snow and put our heads very close to the burrow mouth and sniff and listen. Sometimes we have been able to hear, as if from a great distance underground, faint thumpings and scrabblings going on. What always seems remarkable to us is that no matter how many of our plumy-tailed, striped neighbors, each equipped with a fearful stench supply, may be fitfully dozing together and jostling one another deep down there somewhere under the witch-hazel roots, the skunk smell we can detect at the tunnel mouth is not even as strong as the drift of musk at a fox den. Our neighbor *Mephitis* in wintertime, huddled in the underground warmth in the company of his skunk-kind, must be even more mild-spirited and placidly equable than ever.

Usually by February, sometimes earlier in easy winters, our skunks have dispersed from their winter den. Mary and I find skunk tracks almost every day now when we go exploring our outdoors—wandering little tracks that go erratically up the wood road, tracks along our lane between the thawing snow banks, tracks of skunks that have made an enormous night journey (enormous for such short little legs, and such slow travelers)—all the way up the hill and across four or five fields in a wavering circle and then back down again. *Mephitis* is ordinarily not much of a journeyer. For all the wandering erratic course his excursions follow, he is likely to keep puttering and rocking along for a whole night without ever going more than a few hundred yards from his place of beginning. But in February the mating instinct seizes small *Mephitis,* and in his search for female skunks he greatly broadens his customary territory.

February and March, in the part of the country where Mary and I have our neighborhood, are ordinarily snowy months, even though, as I was saying a while ago, we count them as spring, not winter. In this season of their earliest activity, skunks, of course, cannot find many of the innumerable items of diet—crickets, grasshoppers, birds' eggs, cicadas, beetles, earthworms, bees, and some dozens of other things—that make their foraging in mild seasons such an easy and effortless undertaking. As a skunk goes puttering along through the presolstice snows, he has to content himself largely with such foods as frozen buds and berries, the woody fungi that grow on old stumps, and the occasional dormant insects or insect larvae he may discover by scratching away loose bark or overturning small stones. It is in this snowy season of earliest spring or prespring that skunks most often turn up in poultry houses, the grave little mind and hunger-pinched little stomach of *Mephitis* having been touched by the vision of a warm egg. For the skunks of Mary's and my neighborhood, this is the season when skunk thought turns to the naturalists' woodshed.

The calendar of earth events, by which Mary and I live and which has become profoundly meaningful to us over our years of living with the same animals, the same birds, the same trees and wildflowers and flowing brook, the same living landscape as continual companion, has in it certain special or festival days, as does any calendar. These days, for us, have nothing to do with Washington's Birthday or Election Day, or with those more venerable observances relating to such events as the death at Arian hands of Eusebius of Samosata. What marks off the rounds and rhythms of the life of such naturalists as us is the return of the phoebe to our old barn, the formation of the first autumn ice crystals on a brook pool layered with yellow elm leaves, the day we hear the first spring peepers calling from the marsh—things like that. There is the day when suddenly our old farmhouse is filled with a low, voluminous, thudding, beating sound, not so much a sound, really, as a sort of shuddering, like the shuddering in a church structure when the organ powerfully plays a note almost too low to be heard as sound. It is impossible to localize; it is as though the air were being beaten by invisible wings. "Chim-

ney swifts are back in the chimney!" cries Mary; and we
grow still together, and take this to us, in a moment of the
earth calendar that is a great event. There is the day of First
Frost. There is the day of First Thaw. There is the day of Sap
Running. There is the tremendous earth occasion, or at least
we think it tremendous, when Mary wades out through the
snowdrifts to her garden buried under the whiteness and cries
"Snowdrops are out!" There are always snowdrops planted in
Mary's garden in recollection of the earliest Irish gardens she
knew; and the day their tiny white flowers, on their frail little
stems, come thrusting up impossibly through the snow and
the frozen mulch is a day in our outdoors calendar of late winter that is as meaningful to us as the drawing near of the
solstice itself. Of all the many days of special significance to
naturalists like us, around the year, there is none we enjoy
more, or can count on more dependably, than our day of
Skunk-in-Woodshed.

On an evening in the snowy February-March season, the
time of our year that Indians, with their continual awareness
and sympathetic understanding of animal lives around them,
used to designate as the Hunger Moon, we are sitting quietly
together in our house and suddenly the stillness is broken by
a sound that has come to be as eloquent to us of this season as
is the change of our chickadees' wintry-staccato *chickadee-
dee-dee!* to the long-drawn soft *pheeeeee-beeee!* presaging
spring.

Thwock-thwock-bump. Thwock-thwock-bump.

250

We look at each other and smile a large pleased smile.

The noise is being made by the drawing back and releasing of the screen door between our kitchen and the woodshed. Small, dark, heavy-clawed paws are scratching and fumbling at the door until it is pulled open a few inches, and then letting go of it so that it makes a bumping clattery slam. Like most else in a country house built during the administration of President Millard Fillmore, the doorway from our kitchen to our woodshed is considerably out of plumb; so the closing door, instead of making one brief, neat *bang* when it is shut, makes a long diminuendo of them: *thwock-thwock-bump-bump-bump,* like the muffled clatter of a drumming grouse in far-away woods.

Thwock-thwock-bump-bump-bump. We hear the sound again as if in increased urgency.

The hidden pit up in our woods, among the birches and aspens, evidently has failed to provide enough edible odds and ends. It is a raw, cold, snow-blown night, and bits of icy fungus and winter-pinched berries do not have much warming comfort for a small stomach suffering the emptiness of long weeks of drowsy den-up. Our neighbor *Mephitis* has turned to us, as every year at this season, for a share of our table.

It would be a sentimentality, of course, to think that our skunk visitor in the woodshed purposely rattles and slams the door to call us. No doubt he just fumbles and fiddles with the old door in the random, puttering skunk way in which he investigates everything else. It is curious, all the same, how *Mephitis* manages to make exactly the same noise every year and, as we have found experimentally on two or three occasions of ignoring it for a while to see what would happen, how he keeps it up and keeps it up until we respond. As I said earlier, a skunk has only a negligible voice. He is one of the most silent of our animal neighbors. If not by design, then by curious coincidence, he manages on each Hunger Moon visit to our house to achieve a remarkably effective signaling.

Mary and I go to the kitchen and switch on the woodshed light, and Mary undertakes her annual role as skunk-provider.

It would not be true to say that Mary likes skunks even better than any other animal neighbor with whom we have achieved intimacy in the years in our small world. She likes them all and has enough insighted affection to spare so that she can even feel a kind of gingerly comradeliness with the chunky-bodied, blotch-marked water snake that lazes away the summers on the projecting elm-tree root over the nearest brook pool. But toward amiable little *Mephitis,* so self-contained, so intent on his quiet little skunk preoccupations, so affably rocking along through the woods world with no fiercer thought than finding a cricket and being left alone— toward this little animal neighbor of ours she feels the special fondness that goes out to the misunderstood. Mary makes a point and prerogative of being the one to feed our woodshed visitor.

In the dim illumination of the woodshed's single light bulb, we see a small black-and-white figure, trailing a plume of brushy tail straight out behind him, prowling anxiously back and forth over the earth floor. He sniffs at the woodpile, which must be redolent to his sharp little nose of the legions of our White-foot neighbors who scamper and build their nests in this cobwebby place, and thrusts a tentative paw into chink after chink between the logs. He rises up on short hind legs and pokes tentatively at the lid of the big metal canister in which I keep sunflower seed and suet. He pauses and looks up hopefully as the screen door swings open and Mary steps out to him with a handful of strips of bacon. I stand in the doorway and watch.

Years ago, in our first spring skunk-feedings, Mary used to hold out the bits of bacon (or the bread crusts, or whatever) for *Mephitis* to take them from her fingers. But we found that skunks don't like to take their food this way. What a skunk likes to do is to bat a morsel to the ground with his forepaws and then pinion it firmly while he nibbles and munches. Very quietly and gently, never making any quick move that might be startling to her guest and lead to the catastrophe of a misunderstanding, Mary advances into the woodshed, crouches down, lays a bacon strip on the earth, and murmurs to *Mephitis* such prelanguage sounds of friendly reassurance as may be common both to the dawn of Celtic prehistory and the aboriginal psyche of a small animal with dark striped fur. His always waddling gait quickening to what is fairly a jiggle of pleasure, *Mephitis* comes to her. Pinning her offering with both forepaws, he falls to plucking and munching. Mary stays stone-still, crouched beside him.

Two pieces of bacon, three, four—then very gradually Mary straightens up.

"No more, Skunk. No more now. No more tonight."

She spreads her hands in the gesture of emptiness, while a pair of dark little eyes looks intently at her and makes I-don't-know-what of it. In a minute or two *Mephitis* wheels away and slips through the woodshed door and out into the snowy night. We watch him until he is out of sight, ambling and shuffling vigorously along, his skunk spirit assuaged, his small stomach warmly stuffed with bacon.

Our season of Skunk-in-Woodshed usually lasts about two weeks, with *Mephitis* sometimes coming to us every night, sometimes only every second or third night, but always with the *thwock-thwock-bump* announcement at the screen door and always with the same grave, happy ritual taking place in the dim light by the dusty log pile. Then four or five nights pass and we have no visitor, and we know that this particular great event of our earth calendar is over for another year. Skunks are mating and founding their families now; and furthermore the Hunger Moon is giving place to the Waken-ing Moon, which means that our brook is losing its sheath of ice, all sorts of buds and tender twig tips are becoming avail-able in the woods, and, above all, the thaws are making it easy again for puttering *Mephitis* to paw out meadow mice.

I put down "End of Skunk-in-Woodshed" in our record book, and Mary and I take to listening for the first wild, sweet callings of killdeers over the thawing fields and the first soft songs of bluebirds in the old apple trees in our orchard.

Our next intimate meeting with *Mephitis* is usually not until well into the summer.

As the spring advances, of course, we meet occasional ambling skunk neighbors on their leisurely errands in the lengthening evenings, and we usually find at least one burrow where a skunk family is being raised. There is a big old oak stump, a few dozen yards from our lane on the uphill side in the dense growth of twenty-year-old maples, where almost every year a new skunk generation comes into being. But the hollow under the stump runs very far back into the sidehill, so far that we have not been able to have a close-up look at the infant skunklets in the very earliest period of their lives. As I walk for the mail on spring mornings, I often detour through this piece of woods to pass near the skunks' oak-stump house, and occasionally I meet mother skunk prowling and puttering nearby. The four or five babies she is nursing in the nest chamber deep inside the burrow take a considerable time in their maturing. A newborn skunk is as blind, helpless, and pink a little mite of animalness as one of our baby cottontails, though from the first there shows a faint tracing on the pink crinkled skin of the black-and-white striping that will mark adulthood. For a long period at the beginning of his life, a baby skunk is unseeing. His eyes do not open until he is about three weeks old.

Then it takes him several more weeks to grow sturdy enough to go rocking and trundling forth from the burrow mouth for his first explorations of the world in his mother's wake. Young *Mephitis,* carrying the unique protective weapon he does, is under no urgent necessity to mature quickly, leave home, and learn wary ingenuities for survival in the woods world. I cannot remember whether it was in connection with skunks or some other animal that an old naturalist of my boyhood once used a phrase that sticks in my mind; but the words apply to our neighbor *Mephitis* perfectly. "He does not need to be quick. Nature is quick for him."

As spring passes into summer, Mary and I watch for a skunk parade. There is no other way to describe the excursions of a mother skunk with her brood.

Naturalists have sometimes suggested that the origin of sea-serpent legends may lie in observations of a single-file group of playing water animals, probably porpoises, the curves of whose backs, one behind the other in a spaced chain as the animals dive cavorting, look like the loops or undulating segments of a single animal's very long body. In this same way, a group of swimming otters often looks remarkably like one impossibly long otter, an otter water snake. The land version of this illusion is provided by a family of our neighbor *Mephitis* out for a parade through our meadows and pasture on a summer evening.

In the late dusk, Mary and I are sitting quietly on an old stone wall, or perhaps just walking very slowly through the twilight, watching for a glimpse of Whitetail or fox, listening to the last thrush songs and the first calling of owls in the dark trees at the woods edge.

"Look! Here come our skunks!"

An area of the tall field grass, we see, is being stirred and ruffled as though a breeze were passing through it, creating a long serpentine disturbance among the stems. But there is no breeze. In the still evening, as we watch, the line of the long track becomes more and more marked, drawing closer to us; and it is exactly as though some immensely elongated creature were twisting and thrusting its way through the waving grasses. We freeze to complete stillness and wait.

In a few moments our skunk file comes into view.

Mother skunk is rocking and waddling along at her customary absorbed putter, thrusting her nose into likely tussocks, pawing and scrabbling at a stone, turning continually to right or left in mazy skunk meandering. Behind her, spaced out in single file, comes her troop of skunklets—three, four, five of them, sometimes as many as eight. They are exact miniatures of herself, with plumy tails, sedate rocking waddle, heads held close to the earth. They troop along in puttering solemn mimicry of their mother's every action, sniffing and pawing, following every twist and turn of the trail she makes through the tall grass. Though so young and inexperienced in the ways of the green world, they already have the enormous placid calm of skunks. Nothing hurries them, nothing turns them aside, nothing intrudes into

257

their bland preoccupied saunter in their mother's paw-steps through the fragrant field. They have their heritage and they repose in it.

Mild and equable as our neighbor *Mephitis* is, a mother skunk with her little ones is perhaps a little readier than usual to interpret the startling as threatening, so Mary and I don't try to approach close to one of these skunk parades or caravans. But we can be sure that if we stay still there is always at least a good chance that the skunks will bring about the closeness themselves. The long rippling wake in the grass is likely to cover a field, back and forth, back and forth, quite thoroughly in the course of an hour. Staying motionless, we hope that in the course of its erratic prowl the family will come by where we are. It quite often does. We have had a mother skunk and her trail of babies go waddling and rocking past us, lost in their contentments, so close that I could easily have stretched out a hand and seized one of the youngsters by his plumy tail. It has been a temptation almost irresistible. But I found out in a boyhood adventure with a skunk family that even a very small skunk has his equipments, and that, though it is by and large true (though not invariably) that if you pick up a skunk by his tail he is unable to loose his stench, you then face the dismaying problem of how you are to let your outraged little captive go again. I have succumbed to the temptation to catch a woodchuck youngster in my hand, cheerfully paying, for the lovely minute of holding this furry little animal neighbor of ours in such closeness and feeling the beat of his small wild heart, the price of a bone-bitten finger. But a snatched *Mephitis* has a higher price. Mary and I let our winding family of striped neighbors go their way unmolested, and just take our happiness in seeing the wake of them go rippling off through the evening grass into the darkness.

On those uncommon occasions when a skunk is so intolerably provoked that he rouses from his mild absorption in cricket-catching and stump-scrabbling and brings into use his mephitic defense weapon, his performance has almost always the same pattern. Mary and I have seen several explosions occur over the years—not counting that special one, the death-struggle explosion when one of our little neighbors was seized by a great horned owl on the rocky ledge—and *Mephitis's* behavior varies very little. An encounter we watched on a summer evening a few years ago between a skunk and a big woodchuck was altogether characteristic.

We were in my workroom in the old barn. Daytimes, in summer, this is where I do my writing. It used to be a wagon shed; and now, not greatly adapted, it makes a place where I can work on my chronicling of nature adventurings and reflections to the congenial accompaniment of White-foot neighbors pattering on the old beams, a phoebe eyeing me from her mossy nest on the bracket under the eaves, and old Frolic and Dan every now and then coming to rest their chins on the window sill and breathe their grassy breaths over my shoulder. The window of this barn workroom looks out into the orchard and pasture, with a glimpse of the brook and the far woods. During the daytime, of course, I try not to pay too much attention to the animal events occurring in this small scene, though every now and then a morning's or afternoon's work goes undone because a woodchuck neighbor, ten feet from my typewriter, does something so curious or unfamiliar that I get lost in watching and thinking about it, or the phoebe is menaced, as she once was, by a milk snake gliding toward her nest along an old rafter over my head, or I have a corner-of-the-eye glimpse of a fox over at the edge of the woods, or whatever. For the most part, I try to shut off, during working hours, my notice of such particulars. But on summer evenings Mary and I often spend some hours in this barn room, frankly relaxed in animal-watching enjoyments. It makes a good watching place on those evenings when the mosquitoes render it nearly impossible to spend more than a few minutes in vigil in the woods. We have never seen any very extraordinary animal thing from the barn window, but many quietly pleasant things: a cottontail neighbor eluding a marsh hawk, a woodchuck family playing, the barn swallows skimming and skittering down to the brook in the dusk, and so on. The barn window gave us an excellent chance to watch our neighbor *Mephitis* in an encounter that provoked him to explosion.

We had seen this skunk come puttering up along the brook edge from a clump of sumac whose stems are all rubbed bare by the heifers' shoulders, for this is one of their favorite brook-crossing places; and we had watched him following a typical skunk meander from apple tree to apple tree, from stump to grass tussock, weaving and wandering. Presently he drew near a woodchuck burrow a few feet from the bank of the brook. With an erratic swerve, he went bumbling and lumbering to have a look into it.

At almost the same moment the big rufous-breasted chuck who inhabited this burrow, and who had for the past half-hour or so been browsing around the evening orchard, came galumphing for home at a heavy-footed, rippling run.

Skunk and woodchuck met perhaps two yards from the burrow mouth.

The woodchuck stood still. The skunk stood still, or as still as our neighbor *Mephitis* ever stands. He has a way of jiggling and rocking his body in a continual series of small motions even when he is not walking.

Mary and I watched from the barn window, sure that within a moment or two the woodchuck would yield and leave the skunk to his whims. Almost every animal in the woods and fields understands that *Mephitis* is not to be threatened or challenged. Even bears are careful not to trouble a skunk.

Our woodchuck, however, was in ignorance, or perhaps just caught up uncontrollably in a flare of proprietorship. He edged forward a few inches, reared up, and bared his teeth. We could hear him make a low, squealy growling, deep in his throat.

In the mild, habitual way of skunks, *Mephitis* began delivering his warnings. He lowered his little head, always carried quite close to the ground, in a ducking bob, and slowly he raised his hindquarters higher. He began to make a little clicking, chattering noise with his teeth.

The woodchuck growled again and came forward in a darting rush.

Now the skunk grew ominously still.

With his short forelegs stiffened, he began pattering and thumping the ground with them. It was not unlike the way our skunk imprisoned in the tin can kept lifting and lowering his paws while I worked over him, but with the difference that this was a much quicker and more vigorous motion, like stamping. It is the next-to-last part of the warning that *Mephitis* commonly gives, before loosing, as if in desperate reluctance, his defensive fire.

Now the final warning. Up, up, went the plume of tail, until it stood curved forward over *Mephitis's* back. As its hairs were erected, the tail seemed to swell to at least twice its previous size. It had become a gigantic war plume, seeming so unmistakable in significance that no woodchuck, however ignorant or insistently proprietary, could possibly fail to be given pause.

But the woodchuck charged.

It seemed to both Mary and me probable enough that the woodchuck had no intention to attack *Mephitis,* but only to dash past that obstructive little figure and bolt into his burrow. When once the amiable, preoccupied spirit of a skunk is roused to fighting readiness, however, the slightest further hint of disturbance is enough to touch off the climax. The woodchuck charged forward—and in an instant it happened.

Mephitis wheeled and fired.

The way a scent-firing skunk wheels around is rather hard to describe. It is not a complete turnaround so that he faces away from his target for an instant. He keeps his gaze steadily forward, and his stubby forefeet firmly planted; but he suddenly whips his hindquarters around forward, so that his little striped body is for a second or two bent almost in the drastic curve of a U. Both *Mephitis's* fore end and rear end, in the instant of the discharge, are aimed at the enemy. In the second of this contortion, he everts his scent glands, squeezes powerful posterior muscles, and sends flying the high-pressured jet of his sulfide.

Mary and I could see a glimmering yellow cloud of spray strike the woodchuck and envelop him. He stumbled and lurched in the breath-stopping impact of it, recovered himself, and fled blindly down the burrow. For many seconds after he had disappeared, soaked, choking, blinded, the fine spume of the explosion was still visible to us. Slowly as a patch of fog it settled to earth all around the burrow area, glistening on grass-blades and weed stalks, drenching the soil. The drift of it came rankly to us even through the closed window. The maker of this pestilence had not even paused. The instant the spray had been fired, he had ducked around clear of the hovering fog of it and had gone placidly rambling off in a new direction. We watched him go puttering away through the evening, his tail only gradually lowering as he got farther and farther away from the scene of the encounter and as the thought of it presumably faded from his dim little skunk mind, giving place to customary mild meditations upon grasshoppers and beetles. As he disappeared from sight, around a distant apple tree, his tail was restored to its peaceful position as a horizontal trailing plume. I think it is a safe guess that our little *Mephitis* had by then forgotten all about the episode that had intruded into the quiet of his evening.

The woodchuck, we found, did not forget.

When I went over to the barn to work the next day, there was still a heavy redolence of skunk in my writing room. After I had had the place open to the sun and air for a while, I decided that the smell could be conquered only at its source. So I spent an hour or two shoveling fresh earth over the patch of stench around the woodchuck burrow and piling fresh earth into the burrow mouth itself. This would keep the smell down for a while, at least; and I took it that when things had cleared a bit, the woodchuck would dig his burrow open again.

He never did. One meeting with an outraged skunk had been enough for him. When his eyes had stopped smarting and he could get his breath again, he must have slipped out of his burrow by the bolt-hole back door and moved away to start a fresh burrow in some other part of our pasture entirely.

"Here come our skunks!" calls Mary, on a happy summer evening, and we watch the tall grass part as the serpentine file of our solemn little striped neighbors comes wandering through the meadow.

264

Meeting Mephitis

Thwock-thwock-bump goes an old door in our house on a blowy February night. *Thwock-thump-bump* with renewed insistence.

"Skunk in the woodshed!" cries Mary, and hurries to see if we have bacon to share with a grave little neighbor of ours who is hungry.

Mephitis has his terrible weapon. He has his skunk personality, his sovereignty of self. But also he has his gentleness, his solemn-faced little friendliness, even, as it seemed at least on one occasion, his strangely understanding forbearances. Anyone, man or animal, must respect *Mephitis*. But knowing him as a close neighbor over the years, Mary and I have found our respect ever more and more intermixed with a special affection.

Neighborhood Rewards

Though the world in which Mary and I live is a world of only a hundred-and-some acres, so that in a sense the creation is reduced for us just to sample size—"mountains" become this particular small hillocky mountain with the old wood road climbing up it, the waters of the earth become this particular three-quarters of a mile of winding brook, the land in entirety becomes a land bounded by the "staddle of oak" at its western edge and by the overgrown swamp at its eastern —the companioning animals in such a world are a large company.

266

In a naturalist's broadest sense of the word, of course, they are a company virtually inexhaustible; for "animals" can mean all the kinds of creatures that share the breath of life in "animation." The tawny spangle-winged fritillary butterfly on a thistle top is an animal. The killdeer plover wheeling and crying over the furrowed fields is an animal. It is an animal that Mary and I see when a little red salamander peeps out at us from a cranny in a rotted log in the ferny dampness of our woods; and it is an animal, again, that we meet when we encounter a milk snake in the meadow grass or a shining minnow in a pool of our brook. But even in the common conversational sense of the word animals, which is what Mary and I had in mind when we began writing this book about our countryside and neighbors, our animal intimates are a great many. Every woods adventure I tell reminds me of another one, and that one reminds Mary of a third. Every recollected mood or meditation that has struck us—in the twilight by Muskrat Pool, on a crackling January day as we stood in the hoof-printed snow by a deer bed in our hemlock woods, in a time of silent vigil together in the darkness at our little windows that overlook the pasture and orchard—asks insistently to be included. I have told about our animal-knowings and animal-thinkings together, however, in terms of about as many of our animal neighbors as can well be chronicled without the risk of giving a sense of repetition. To naturalists, of course, there is a gulf of difference between a white-footed mouse and a meadow mouse; and an intimate knowing of

meadow-mouse life in the green tunnels of the fields, however well the life way of White-foot has already been known,
comes with all the delight of novelty. But to anyone not a
naturalist, Mary and I can see, the one kind of mouse and the
other kind of mouse must after all both seem to have a great
deal of the same elements of mousiness; so that our neighbor
White-foot who fills my inkwell with cherry pits is probably
a wise sufficiency of mouse story for one book. White-foot
plus woodchuck plus muskrat adds up to a total beyond which
an account, say, of our neighbor *Tamias striatus,* the chipmunk, must come in a way as more of the same; for though
the four animals differ signally, there are also in their lives
broad areas of impingement. Our *Tamias,* for instance, digs
his concealed burrow hole from underneath in very much the
way our big squirrel neighbors, the woodchucks, do. A woodchuck burrow and a chipmunk burrow and a muskrat burrow are each, to neighborhood naturalists like Mary and me,
extraordinary and special as we go about the discovery and
exploration of them in the vividness of outdoors; but in print,
in the telling, it must come in time to seem that one burrow
is very like another. It is one thing when you sit by the
burrow, in living experience, hearing your chuck neighbor
squealing or twittering down in his underearth house that
smells of roots and rain, watching in the breathless twilight
stillness your muskrat neighbor nibbling a water root while
the moon comes up over the dark woods, but it is another
thing to be reading about this, not being there in the sun-hot

268

pasture or in the dusk by the cool pool; and then it can seem that the excitement of one burrow is hardly to be revived over another one.

I have told about animal neighbors as diverse and rangingly representative as possible in this book, both for this reason and in a hope Mary and I have entertained that there might be conveyed a kind of rounded over-allness in the picture of our animal company, reduced to a fraction though the representation of that company has to be. Animal life, as I have said a good many times in a good many ways in these pages, all goes together. Even the most distant and disparate elements of it are caught in bond. It all has its community. Mary and I live in a microcosmic world, and at least something of this microcosmic quality, if possible, should find expression in a book about our animal neighbors whose lives make up the living texture of it. So I have written about the biggest animal neighbor with whom we share these woods and fields, Whitetail, our deer, and about that one of the littlest animal neighbors, White-foot, our woods mouse, who gnaws bucks' shed antlers; about our cottontails who die in their legions, and the foxes they help support; woodchuck who makes his burrows, and skunk who adapts them; muskrat whose life is interlinked with the life of flowing water, as inextricably as is the life of vegetation which in turn interdepends with woodchuck again, and so on in intricacies to the flowering and flourishing of the whole biota, flatworm in his puddle of water, chickaree, the red squirrel, in his conifer top, black-masked little bear, our raccoon neighbor, dozing in the hollow of the oak.

All the created world, in all its parts and entirety, is a united whole. All creatures in it are in a common brotherhood. Everything is interconnected with everything else. Not only is there a basic brotherhood between a man in England and a man in America, or a man in Antarctica and a man in Siberia, but there is a bond between a man and a mouse, or a tree and a fox, or a frog and a raccoon. We are all participants together in the united entirety of the creation. We are all the creatures of the one parental and primary source of all begetting, whether we may like to call that source nature, or may like to call it something like the life force, or may like to employ the traditional language of religious utterance and use the name of God.

The sense of brotherhood with all our fellow ingredients in the created world is a very old thing, a primitive awareness, a kind of spontaneous poetry going back to earliest dawn days. An aboriginal Indian thought of a bear as his brother. He felt relationship, and thus a kind of family obligation, even to the herbs he gathered and the trees he felled. But the sense of brotherhood, thus felt, is not a merely primitive thing. It has been felt by religious men and aware men in all times. There was St. Francis of Assisi, looking out upon a universe of what he understood to be his fellow creatures, and so saluting with affection his sister, the moon, and his brother ox and his brothers the wolf and the stag and the heron and the rabbit.

This that primitive men and contemplative men have always felt—this brotherhood of all the creation, all brought into being by the same creative agency, all under a responsibility thus both filial and fraternal—is something our kind of naturalist every day sees more and more clearly to be strict fact. All the creatures, of which we are but one, are brotherly components in the one whole of nature. We share a grandfather with owls and with the striped dace that swim in our creek. We have a family link with the oak tree that towers on the hill. We are the brother of a woodchuck, and the brother of a small *Mephitis* with a plumy tail, and the brother of the dark moss that grows on the stone in the forest.

I don't know how much of this can be made to seem livingly real in one small book about some animal neighbors on one small piece of land; but Mary and I have hoped that at least something of it can. It is one of the things we have had in mind in choosing what neighbors to write about, for we have hoped that they might display not only the range and differences of animals, as animals are to be found and known even on one small area of earth over years of neighbor-knowing, but, under that and resolving the separatenesses, the community of wholeness that catches all living things together and relates them in the general melody of earth.

Well now, it is time to call a bookful a bookful and to close this company of our neighbors.

Neighbors, I call them now; and a minute ago I was calling them brothers. It is not a discrepancy. Back at the beginning

of our writing, Mary and I looked up neighbor in an una-
bridged dictionary, to make sure it was the right word for
what our animals have been to us; and we were astonished
and delighted to find that it was even more the right word
than we had guessed. I spoke of this in the first chapter. A
neighbor, says this dictionary, is a nigh dweller; but furthermore, it goes on, the nighness—when neighborliness is carried to its farthest and when the implication of it is exercised
in utmost—becomes such intimacy as to signify blood relationship; it becomes the closeness of cousins; it deepens at
last to brotherhood completely. Neighbor and brother. It is
precisely what every deer is to us, standing drinking at our
brook in the evening, what every coon is to us, trundling
along and churring in the night, paw-printing the black loam
of our brook bank with his flat little-child's soles, what every
animal we know and love is, from the towering buck tossing
his head on the high east ridge to tiny White-foot sneezing
and polishing his whiskers in the glow of our bedside lamp.
The understanding that to know neighbor-close is to be
brought to brotherhood, that to "possess" animals in this intimacy is to find them bone of your bone, even, in their fashion,
mind of your mind—this is the whole reason really why this
book is this book, and why, as Mary and I think, neighborhood naturalists are the naturalists they are, and why for all
our years together it has never seemed to us depriving or
lonely, but on the contrary fulfilling and companionable to
live ten miles out on R.F.D. from the post office and to have

our little road closed with the snows of every winter. Neighbor and brother. Let this stand just so; for in a phrase it is everything Mary and I have to say, and what our life is.

Someone once said to Henry Thoreau, commenting on his life in the woods, that it must be a lonely experience.

"Lonely?" said Thoreau, in his quirky, cranky way. "Lonely? Why should I be lonely? Is not our planet in the Milky Way?"

A naturalist's sense of community with all the rest of the living, breathing fellowship of beings may not often expand, in such a high mystical gesture as this, to include vegetations, rocks, waters, and the most distant glitter of star in the night sky. But it is the sense of this recognition, at least in some degree, that does give any naturalist a great part of his reward; and it is the possibility of making the fellowship an ever closer intimacy, of taking the reality of it so entirely to you that, as it were, you can hold it in your possessing hand—warm with the warmth of a woodchuck youngster, damp with the dewy dampness on the felted blanket over a nest of baby cottontails, quivering and life-pulsing with the tremulousness of a little fawn nibbling at your finger in a summer dusk—that makes a certain kind of naturalist choose to be a neighborhood naturalist.

The world in which Mary and I live, and which we explore continually in our adventures in possession, is a small world and in a way an isolated world in its cleft in the hills. I suppose it could be said to us: It must be a lonely world. A thing we

have wanted to do in this book, along with telling about the
life ways of a variety of our neighbors, is to say why it is not.

Omitting the times of exalted insight, the expansions into
that awareness when the farthest star is close as a brother and
the thud of your own blood is in family relation with the
arterial beat of the seasons, there are continual companionings
in this kind of life and this kind of small world. Lonely? How
can it be lonely? Is there not a raccoon teetering out on a
maple-tree twig and peeking in at the window? Are there
not woodchucks enjoying their woodchuck contentments all
across the sunny pasture and foxes pattering along the trails
through the sweet fern and hawthorn to Fox Crossing?
Listen: that is our neighbor Whitetail, coughing and snorting
over in the birch copse. Watch: there is the drift of a little
bundle of water grasses, down the brook, that says our neighbor muskrat is just around the bend, plunging and gliding in
his sleek delights. Sniff at the morning air now, on this day
of February: this is the musk of *Mephitis,* aprowl with spring.
What a neighborhood naturalist can never be is lonely, for
neighbor lives are all around him and his life is caught up in
their lives, his excitement participating in their excitements,
his spirit gone outside his personal periphery to a sharing
with them. Lonely? Not when there is a little skunk gravely
eating his bacon, Mary would say. Not when a coon and I
enjoy the same chocolate bar, between the barn and the brook,
in a profound community in the glimmering darkness. Not
when all around us there is the sight and sound of our neigh-

bors, the acts and meanings of their neighbor lives to be taken to us, the lilt and going forward of all this to be entered into and shared with a blood-and-bone fellowship around all the seasons.

A naturalist has two possible worlds for contemplation. One of them is a very large world, the planetary world, this spherical earth of ours, as it might be seen by one standing off somewhere in outer space and taking in the view of the whole slowly turning, slowly circling ball of star clay with all its teeming freight of creatures. In this huge all-over and far-stretching view, a naturalist's look encompasses the hippopotamuses lazing in their African mud wallow, the foxes capering under the moon in snowy New England pastures, sea birds wheeling and crying around the Orkneys, bats in Panama, dingoes in Australia, a garden slug on a Sussex vine. This sweeping view of the whole pageant and parade of animaldom is also a tremendous time view: aeon after geological aeon passing, as it were, under the observer's eye, from the first stir in the first earth slime to the Now of the rising sun this morning. This world of a naturalist's contemplation has at least three million different species of animals in it, at least fifteen thousand species of birds, more than two thousand species of the creatures called snakes. This naturalist's world is huge, thronged, and stretches in space and time for gigantic distances.

The second world for a naturalist's contemplation is a very different world. It is the world into which he may step, as one

275

going on a safari, by just opening his front door. It is the
world, perhaps only a half-mile long and a quarter-mile wide,
of his own woods and fields, in which, instead of a thronging
multitude of such strange beasts as elephants and auks, there
is perhaps to be found at a given moment only the one familiar
mammal, a woodchuck, or the one homely bird, a sparrow or
a bluejay. This second world for a naturalist's contemplation
is the immediate world of here and now: nature reduced to
smallness and intimacy, the parade and pageant of animaldom become just *this* animal, in the dusk at Muskrat Pool,
on the rocky ledge by the Pileated Tree, the time view con-
tracted to just now, this instant.

It is the paradox of a naturalist's situation that the first of
his worlds—the great, grand spreading one, the one that encompasses all lands and seas and skies and forests of all the
earth, and that covers a time span of hundreds upon hundreds
of millions of years—is in a certain sense fairly easy to get to
know a good deal about; whereas the second world, the world
of the actual patch of earth on which his feet stand, the world
of this chipmunk scurrying from the familiar rosebush to the
familiar oak tree, and of that bluejay perching on the weathered fence post and crying *Beadle-beadle!* as it has cried
Beadle-beadle! every morning for months and years, is a
world requiring the devoted observations of a lifetime before
a naturalist can lift himself out of the category of ignoramus.

"The world," meaning the whole of it, can be packaged
after a fashion in a bundle of lore that anybody who has the

taste for it can pretty well acquire in the course of years of reading, study, travel, converse with specialists, and similar modes of acquiring knowledge. But the world of Right Here —this chipmunk, that bird, this earthworm directly beside our shoe sole—well, that world is so small, and can be peered into with such directness, that it is of infinite adventure and excitement and enormous with the unknown. Though the big world, the entirety of nature, is never intimately possess-able because of its vastness, at least the general scheme of it can be acquired in that sound smatter of *scientia* which every naturalist, neighborhood or other sort, must have; and it can happen, with this acquisition, that a naturalist may have a sense of being "finished" or even of being bored. Nothing like this can ever happen in the case of the little world, the world that is only as big as this cow pasture bright with buttercups and thistles, this little area of woods where the thrushes are singing. Nothing like this can happen in the little world where *Mammalia* (that huge abstraction, but textbook-learnable, even perhaps eventually tedious) is suddenly re-duced to this focused blaze of living reality, quivering and in-calculable, this intimate astonishment, this neighbor, this White-foot who is sitting on your worktable with a cherry stone in his paws.

Like so many other things I have tried to say in these pages, this thing that Mary and I feel about being neighborhood naturalists is very hard to say. Probably, in the end, it is un-sayable. It is wisest, I guess, just to hope that the hint of it

277

may come through, if by indirection, in what we have told about some of our adventurings and thinkings together.

What Mary and I find the reward of living in a country neighborhood, taking the creation to us in little, taking our animals to us not simply as species of creatures but as neighbor beings, may not be possible to say. But it can be lived, we know. A few minutes ago, over at the edge of the hemlock and hickory woods beyond the southern highland of the pasture, we heard a great hubbub of crows crying "Fox! Fox!" There is some exciting thing happening over there, something new for us to learn, some opportunity to take closer and closer to us the being of a neighbor of ours and to deepen our possession of the world.